Ideology, Politics,
and Government in
the Soviet Union

Ideology, Politics, and Government in the Soviet Union

AN INTRODUCTION

Revised Edition

John A. Armstrong

FREDERICK A. PRAEGER, *Publishers*
New York · Washington · London

FREDERICK A. PRAEGER, PUBLISHERS
111 Fourth Avenue, New York, N.Y. 10003, U.S.A.
5, Cromwell Place, London S.W.7, England

Published in the United States of America in 1967
by Frederick A. Praeger, Inc., Publishers

This is a revised and expanded edition of the book published
in 1962 by Frederick A. Praeger, Inc., Publishers.

Second printing, 1968

© 1962, 1967 by Frederick A. Praeger, Inc.

Library of Congress Catalog Card Number: 67-20470

This book is Number 113 in the series
Praeger Publications in Russian History and World Communism

Printed in the United States of America

To Roy and Leona Taylor

PREFACE
TO THE REVISED EDITION

When I wrote the first edition of this book five years ago, I believed there was a need for a brief, simplified survey of the main features of the Soviet political system. Since that time, the reception given the book suggests that it has, indeed, served a purpose. I am convinced that a good part of the book's utility has been due to its timeliness. The first edition appeared less than a year after the Twenty-second Congress of the Soviet Communist Party; Nikita Khrushchev was then apparently at the height of his power. Khrushchev has since been displaced by a "collective leadership" of oligarchs. The confident progress toward Communism predicted by the program adopted at the Twenty-second Congress has been de-emphasized. Innumerable institutional changes have taken place. Some of these new developments represent trends envisaged in the first edition, nevertheless, the changes have been such that that edition has ceased to provide a reliable, comprehensible introduction. Yet, I am more than ever convinced that such an introduction is needed by students in interdisciplinary programs dealing with Russia, by students in general comparative government courses, and even by students beginning specialized study of the Soviet political system.

The second edition has been almost completely revised so as to provide an introduction focusing on *current* Soviet politics. As with the first edition, for the sake of brevity I have omitted almost all history of Soviet institutional development and political rivalry from this volume. Government in the Soviet

Union is no longer a curiosity, and only in a very special sense can one describe it as an experiment. Consequently, a preliminary look at the system may well take for granted its relative stability, its capacity as a going concern. It seems to me that the historical examination of political institutions and behavior can reasonably be postponed. The great danger of this type of approach is the loss of historical perspective. I have tried to avoid, or at least limit, this danger by treating the more remote background of present-day Soviet society in the opening chapter. Furthermore, while institutions and behavior can be presented out of their historical context, the same does not hold true for Soviet ideology, which is incomprehensible except in its developmental framework. Consequently, Chapter 2, though not chronological in organization, contains numerous references to the precursors of the present Soviet ideologues.

Both aspects of the historical background just mentioned are part of what social science theorists increasingly agree on calling "political culture." During the past five years, the conceptual framework and vocabulary of systems analysis and structural functionalism have rapidly become part of the common fund of knowledge of social science students. Even those who do not intend to acquire specialized competence in analytic social science have frequently obtained at least a general familiarity with the approaches. Five years ago it seemed inadvisable to assume any knowledge of a special terminology; today, I believe, occasional references to systems analysis and structural functionalism will help many readers integrate their study of the Soviet system into broader social science study. At the same time, I must hasten to add, I do not feel able to use either of these conceptual frameworks (or a combination of them) as *the* perspective for presenting Soviet politics. I think there is widespread agreement that, of all major categories of political systems, the totalitarian type is least readily susceptible to systems analysis and still less to structural functional analysis. Both approaches were developed primarily from the consideration of pluralist societies like the United States or from the adaptation of anthropological perspectives on traditional societies. The application of these approaches to an extremely centralized political system, dominated by a small, relatively homogeneous elite adhering to an ideology demanding the complete transformation of human nature, requires fundamental reconsideration. The organic analogies behind some of the newer social science models, which tend to assume the existence of unconscious social processes tending toward an equilibrium state, are particularly hard to relate to the highly self-conscious goal orientation of a Communist elite. Eventually, these difficulties may well be overcome. At present, a number of highly interesting attempts to adapt systems and functionalist approaches to totalitarian systems are under way, but I doubt that these adaptations have reached the point at which it is wise to use any of them as the basic organizing principle for an introductory presentation. Consequently, while endeavoring to show the relevance of the newer concepts, I have retained the generally eclectic organization of the first edition. Only on the nationalities question (Chapter 6), where I have recently had the opportunity to adapt functionalist theory in an extended and more rigorous monograph, do I use a highly analytic approach as the basic organizing principle.

At the same time, I must emphasize (as I did in the introduction to the first edition) that a dominantly legal or institutional approach to the study of the Soviet system would be utterly misleading. Emphasis on the constitutional system of Soviet government, or even on the formal structure of the Communist Party of the Soviet Union, would be inappropriate. Consequently, I have confined myself to brief explanations of what I consider to be the significance of formal structure in both government and Party. Additional details on these structures are contained in the organizational charts accompanying the text.

These charts are not confined to the formal structures of Party
and government, but attempt to suggest the dynamics of power
relations as well as formal lines of subordination. In a short
book, illustrations of this kind are exceptionally important.
But even the most penetrating elucidation of structural features could not furnish complete insight into the extent of
Soviet totalitarianism. Such insight requires an understanding
of the complex nationality question, the background of police
terror, and the pervasive control of the economy. Brief as my
treatment is, I have felt it essential to devote nearly a third of
the book to these subjects.

I hope that this work will serve as a useful elementary guide
to the Soviet political system; it is not a compendium of the
opinions of others, or even an abridgment of my own. I have
drawn heavily upon scholarly studies of the Soviet Union;
those I consider most useful for the general reader and non-
specialized student are listed at the end of each chapter. But
the emphasis and many of the conclusions advanced are my
own; no other writer on the Soviet system will accept all of
them without reservation. I am convinced that it is impossible
to avoid a personal approach if one is to present a coherent
analysis of Soviet politics and government, and it should be
pointed out that much of what is said in this book is not established beyond dispute. I have tried to indicate the most important points where the accuracy of available data is doubtful or
where divergence of informed opinion exists, but conciseness
of expression may, at times, have led to unwarranted generalizations. Some readers may question my evidence for certain
statements. Elaborate footnotes seemed out of place in so brief
a survey. Where feasible, I have indicated my sources, such as
the proceedings of the Twenty-second and the Twenty-third
Soviet Communist Party Congresses, in the text. My larger
work, *The Politics of Totalitarianism: The Communist Party
of the Soviet Union from 1934 to the Present* (New York: Ran-

dom House, 1961), provides extensive documentation for the period before these congresses. Evidence for the analysis of recent Party transformation is provided in my article "Party Bifurcation and Elite Interests" (*Soviet Studies,* XVII [April, 1966], pp. 417–30); my recent intensive analysis of Soviet nationalities is cited in full in Chapter 6.

Probably the general reader is more likely to be concerned with over-all information about the workings of the Soviet political system than he is with my particular sources. A major portion of our information on Soviet politics and government is derived from "overt" Soviet sources—for the most part Soviet publications. Even the neophyte will find that the Soviet press provides a revealing, if distorted, reflection of the totalitarian system at work. The reader who wishes to cover a comprehensive range of Soviet publications must know Russian (and, if possible, some of the other languages of the U.S.S.R.). Fortunately, the weekly *Current Digest of the Soviet Press* (351 Riverside Drive, New York, N.Y.) provides English-language translations from an immense range of Soviet publications. The coverage provided by the *Current Digest,* which a single scholar can hardly match, has been indispensable in preparing this book. But I cannot stress too strongly that the beginning student of Soviet affairs should not overrate his ability to understand and appraise Soviet press reports, whether in Russian or in translation. Soviet writings on general subjects, and particularly articles on political affairs, while somewhat more candid in recent years, are geared to propaganda. After a time, the student readily recognizes the propaganda "line" and learns to discount it. It is not so easy to detect the bias of factual "examples" or statistics carefully selected for their propaganda effect. As a rule, only specialists, after painstaking comparative analysis of Soviet materials appearing at different times and places, can extrapolate the facts behind such distorted selection. But the Soviet press is not only a propaganda medium; it is also a functional medium of communication in a highly complex technological society. There are facts to be discovered behind the distortion, for there is a limit to the extent to which Soviet readers can be misled without reducing the effectiveness of their service to the regime. Increasingly, the Soviet regime appears to recognize the significance of this limit; as a result, published information on economic, social, and demographic subjects has become more abundant and diversified as well as more candid.

When internal political rivalries are at issue, however, the Soviet propagandist continues to put up a second screen between the reader and significant developments. This screen consists of "esoteric language"—the use of terms and allusions that the uninitiated fail to understand. In order to grasp the importance of esoteric language, one must have an extensive detailed knowledge of Communist history from before the Revolution to the present. Even with such knowledge, unraveling the meaning of esoteric language is often a matter of educated guess; but such guesses are crucially important in understanding Soviet political developments.

Our ability to penetrate the Soviet communication screens has been immensely helped by occasional access to hidden sources of information. During World War II, the Germans captured a number of extremely important secret documents, including the economic plan for 1941, the archives of a provincial Party organization, and thousands of political directives to guerrillas and regular military units. In 1945, the United States forces seized these materials. Since the end of the war, only a few Soviet secret documents have come to light, but, on occasion, Soviet defectors who had memorized fairly extensive outlines of major documents—such as the secret letters of the Party's Central Committee—have furnished valuable information. Naturally, defectors were most numerous during the war, when the Soviet control system was disrupted. Social scientists (of the Harvard Project on the Soviet Social System) could even construct a sample reflecting the attitudes and backgrounds of the general Soviet population on the basis of interviews with defectors.

Since the mid-1950's, defectors have ceased to be a major source of information on contemporary Soviet internal politics. On the other hand, foreigners, including specialists on Soviet affairs from the United States and Western Europe, have been allowed some direct access to the Soviet Union. While all such visitors have been restricted to a considerable degree, they have obtained a "feel" for the Soviet system, which has helped them draw conclusions from the other sources described above. Exchange students have been able to study series of local newspapers unavailable outside the U.S.S.R. and, sometimes, even to interview Soviet officials. No one who studies the Soviet system intensively would claim that any one of these sources, or even all of them taken together, are fully satisfactory. The social scientist dealing with the U.S.S.R. lacks many "tools," such as survey research on public opinion, that his counterparts concerned with the United States and Western Europe have developed to a high degree. Yet in some ways, the Soviet specialist has an advantage, for he is dealing with a system where decisions are highly centralized and where all general media reflect, however obscurely, the central manipulation. If one can but find the clue, Soviet totalitarian politics may become easier to interpret than the baffling flux that culminates in the expression of the popular will under democratic pluralism.

It should be clear by this point that my principal debt is to the objective scholars and observers who have sifted the great mass of material dealing with Soviet political affairs. Without the numerous systematic studies that already exist, no summary treatment could even be attempted. I am particularly indebted to my colleagues in the University of Wisconsin Russian Area Studies Program for suggestions, and to those elsewhere who have used and criticized the first edition of this book. I am particularly grateful to Robert Campbell for his incisive critique of the draft of Chapter 7 of the revised edition. Again, however, I must stress that the manner of the treatment and the conclusions are my own, and I must consequently bear full responsibility for them. Frederick A. Praeger first suggested the writing of a concise study of this type; to him and his competent editorial staff the work owes a great deal indeed. Lastly, I must acknowledge my great debt to my wife, who not only typed the manuscripts of both editions, but made innumerable improvements in both text and illustrations.

J. A. A.

Department of Political Science
University of Wisconsin
1967

CONTENTS

xv

MAPS, CHARTS, AND TABLES

Ideology, Politics,
and Government in
the Soviet Union

MAP OF

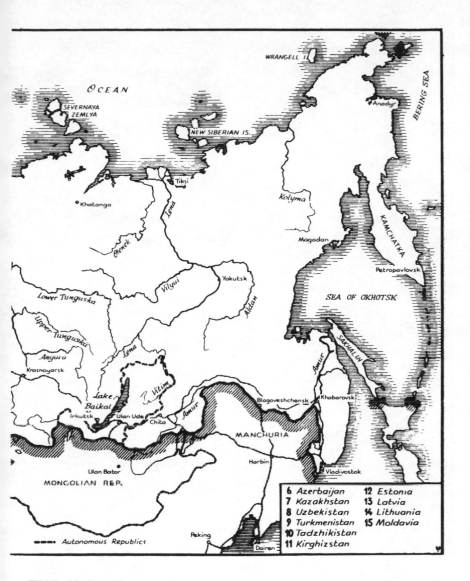

THE U.S.S.R.

1

THE BACKGROUND

At the heart of all political systems is a paradox: political power is based on, and in fact requires, the monopoly of force in a given territory, yet force alone is an inadequate basis for a political system. The paradox is frequently resolved by explaining that the monopoly entails only the *legitimate* exercise of force. But what is legitimate depends on the attitudes of the population of the territory, or at least on the attitudes of a dominant element among the population. Attitudes reflect widely held expectations concerning proper political behavior. Taken together, customs and beliefs constitute the political culture of a society. Ordinarily, the effort to determine the political culture involves direct surveys of the attitudes of the population. In a closed system like the Soviet, this approach is forbidden. Instead, one must rely on two indirect sources for understanding Soviet political culture. To a far greater extent than most political systems, the Soviet system is the creation of a consciously articulated body of ideas—the ideology. We shall look at this ideology in Chapter 2 and, at many points in this book, we shall try to assess its influence on the political culture. But political culture, like most popular beliefs and customs, is extremely persistent. The Soviet ideology has enjoyed a near monopoly in public expression during the past fifty years. Nevertheless, it is highly likely that earlier influences, transmitted by word of mouth, by reading the classic Russian literature, and by unconscious family customs, continue to permeate political culture in the U.S.S.R.

In the following pages, those elements of the Russian past

that seem to be related to present Soviet political culture will be described. It is impossible to establish direct connections between these aspects of Russian history and Soviet behavior, particularly since the regime explicitly disavows the connection in most instances. Until the mid-1930's, Communist writers maintained that nearly all Russian development before the Bolshevik Revolution of 1917, though a necessary stage of social evolution, was nevertheless an outworn and often shameful memory rather than a proud heritage. Since the mid-1930's, the Soviet regime has been more selective in its evaluation of pre-Revolutionary history; but the essential break with the past remains a major element of Soviet Communist thought. The outside observer, on the other hand, is immediately struck by the similarities as well as the differences between the Soviet system and the Czarist regime that prevailed in much the same territory for centuries prior to the establishment of the U.S.S.R. Since Czarism was essentially a Russian phenomenon, and the Russians remain dominant in the U.S.S.R., this chapter will concentrate on the Russian heritage. Chapter 6 will treat the significantly different heritages of the large non-Russian minorities.

ABSOLUTISM

One of the most striking parallels between Czarism and Bolshevism is the existence of an unusual measure of centralized, unrestricted power in both systems. To the student of government at the beginning of this century, Czarist rule was synonymous with autocracy, as indeed it was in the official parlance of the old regime. It is true that in the twelve years immediately preceding the Bolshevik Revolution, some modifications were introduced in the autocratic system. Although the institution of an elected legislative assembly (Duma) did enable public opinion to exercise some pressure upon the Czar, the government of the Russian Empire remained responsible to him alone. Similarly, if one goes back far enough in the history of the East Slavs—from whom the Russians, along with other nationalities, descended—one finds evidence of embryonic democratic institutions. On the whole, however, Russia has probably had less experience with limited government or representative institutions than any other European country.

Orthodox Church and Czarist State

Prominent among the factors contributing to the absolutistic nature of Russian government was the relation between church and state. The Orthodox faith, to which traditionally an overwhelming majority of Russians have adhered, has been an extremely important element in the country's history—so important, indeed, that some historians (notably Arnold Toynbee) class the Russian Orthodox society as a civilization distinct from that of Western Europe. In the Byzantine Empire, from which the Russians obtained their Christian faith in the late tenth century, Orthodoxy had developed the peculiar institution of "Caesaropapism." In this system, the emperor was both autocratic ruler of the state and supreme head of the church. Consequently, the separation of ecclesiastical and temporal power—whether between Pope and Holy Roman Emperor, or between secular state and church—did not exist. The tension, latent or visible, between these two powers in the West, which prevented either from assuming control of all aspects of life, was largely absent in Byzantium. The Orthodox Church might admonish the ruler, but it had to submit to him and support him, evil though he may have been. This doctrine, transplanted to the East Slavic lands, made the church a bulwark of absolute monarchy, especially after the Czars, in the fifteenth century, proclaimed themselves to be the successors of the Byzantine emperors.

The Influence of Mongol Rule

A second major influence in the development of absolutism —some historians consider it to have been more important than the Orthodox doctrine—was the Mongol invasion of the thirteenth century. Living in the broadest portion of the great Eurasian plain, almost unprotected by natural barriers, the East Slavs were easily subjected by the Mongol cavalry. Aside from destroying or dispersing much of the old East Slavic civilization (which for some time had been on the wane), the Mongol invasion gave rise to new distributions of power in Eastern Europe. Indirectly, the principal Russian beneficiaries of Mongol rule were the princes of Moscow, who became the vassals and lieutenants of the khans. While it is not altogether clear where the Mongol khans found their patterns of rule, they required a degree of self-abasement from their subjects commonly associated with Oriental despotisms. The Muscovite princes adopted many of the despotic attitudes and practices of the Mongol rulers, and these attitudes and practices persisted after the princes obtained a position of equality with the surviving Mongol (or Tatar) khans and ultimately subjugated them.

Western Theories of the Divine Right of Kings

In noting these peculiarly Russian experiences that influenced the rise of Czarist absolutism, one should not lose sight of the importance of Western ideas in the establishment of absolute rule. Probably the high-water mark of Czarist autocracy came under Catherine II (the Great) in the eighteenth century. Catherine was German by birth, and most of the intellectual underpinning for her rule was provided by West Europeans. The era was the culmination of the "divine right" theory of monarchy in the West, a justification for absolute rule that had been developed quite apart from the above-noted influences on Russia. In "perfecting" autocracy in the Russian Empire, Catherine and her immediate predecessors were following the almost predominant model of European statecraft. But the special features of the Russian heritage enabled Czarist reality to approach the model more closely than almost any other European country—and to last far longer.

THE "CLASSLESS" SOCIETY

There is a second feature of the Russian heritage that is not nearly so obvious as absolutism. For centuries, most men took social inequality for granted. Distinctions of wealth, rank, even legal privilege, were widespread. One of the most significant developments of the nineteenth century was the concern with such social stratification. As a rule, the phenomenon was described as a "class" structure, though social thinkers presented, and continue to present, widely varying definitions of "class." To the casual Western observer, the Czarist Empire seems almost the epitome of social stratification. The superficial impression is of a glittering, if rather irresponsible, aristocracy; an intense but morbid intellectual milieu; and a downtrodden though enduring peasantry. There is considerable validity in this picture, but it does not necessarily add up to a class society in the traditional pattern of Western Europe. In fact, a whole school of Russian thinkers of the nineteenth century, the Slavophiles, sharply rejected the idea that Russia had classes at all comparable to those of the West, and many Western historians share this viewpoint.* The Slavophiles, indeed, considered the absence of classes in the Rus-

* The Slavophile school, as the name indicates, fervently admired Slavic (in fact, mainly Russian) traditional culture. It contrasted sharply with the "Western-oriented" school of nineteenth-century Russian thinkers, which regarded emulation of Western Europe as a major basis for progress.

sian Empire to be a significant indication of the superiority of the Russian social order over that of the West, a proof of Russian Orthodoxy's devotion to human brotherhood.

The Nobility

In Western Europe, so the Slavophiles argued, the nobility considered itself to be a true aristocracy. Though usually of the same race and nationality as the rest of its country's population, the nobility had for centuries enjoyed the status of a hereditary privileged class. As a result, the nobles regarded themselves as wholly distinct and superior, entitled to rule and to enjoy the fruits of rule. No doubt there is much that is exaggerated in this argument. But it does seem to reflect a fairly common attitude among a group of West European nobles with whom the Russians were in close contact. Since the early part of the eighteenth century, the Russian Empire had included the Baltic provinces, where a small ruling class of German origin dominated a Latvian and Estonian peasantry. There, to quote a Baltic German noble of a later generation,

> The person of the peasant, as such, was completely in the background. If one considered him at all, for the most part one did so with the sort of inquisitive interest with which one today examines some interesting species of man or beast from unknown lands.*

Such a concept of class differentiation, while extreme, no doubt influenced the Slavophiles' view of the West European nobility's mentality.

In the Russian lands of the Empire, the position of the upper stratum was different. The nobles were indeed legally and factually distinct from the remainder of the population, and they enjoyed many privileges. Unlike the typical Western

---

* Astaf von Transehe-Roseneck, *Die Reform der bäuerlichen Verhältnisse in Livland, 1765–1804* (Strasbourg: Karl J. Trubner, 1890).

noble, however, the Russian noble was essentially a servant of the autocracy. No traditions of family honor or class autonomy shielded him from the full force of absolute rule. Historically, the Czars had made and remade the nobility in accordance with the exigencies of their struggle to strengthen and extend their power. Ivan IV (the Terrible) slaughtered many of the nobles, filling their posts with loyal members of his bodyguard and entourage. Later Czars were somewhat less ruthless, but constantly raised large numbers of new men to the nobility. On the other hand, surviving descendants of the princely families of medieval Russia frequently lived as obscure rustics scarcely distinguishable from the peasants. During the last century of Czarist rule, the equation of nobility with service to the regime was codified by regularly conferring patents of nobility upon all who had attained high rank in the civil or military hierarchy. Those who had attained top ranks were entitled to pass on their noble status to their sons. Thus Ilya Ulyanov, Lenin's father,* became a hereditary noble on attaining the post of school superintendent.

Lenin's career, though extreme, suggests the lack of regard for hereditary class status common among all but a small group of "great" families in the Russian Empire. Instead of a self-conscious ruling group, attached to the sovereign by concepts of feudal loyalty but jealous of their rights even as against the crown, the Russian nobles constituted essentially a bureaucratic order, though initially they derived their material support from landed estates rather than salaries. In the latter part of the nineteenth century, the nobles' importance even as landlords diminished, and except for a select group who turned to social welfare and educational work in the "zemstvos" (provincial boards with limited legal authority), the landowners as a group did not constitute a decisive factor

---

* Vladimir Ilich Ulyanov has gone down in history under the name of "Lenin," originally an underground pseudonym.

in the operation of the imperial regime. The real core of the
Czarist system was the great bureaucracy of the capital, St.
Petersburg (now Leningrad), the military commanders in the
field, the governors and police chiefs of the provinces, and
the church hierarchy. These officials maintained order, secured
obedience to the Czar's commands (which, of course, they
often inspired), and even supervised much of the social and
economic development of the country. These bureaucrats (the
term is used in the sociological rather than the pejorative
sense) were often recruited from older noble families, but they
were shaped by their careers rather than by their origins; and,
as noted above, "new men" were constantly wending their way
upward via the bureaucratic system.

The Peasantry

Juxtaposed to the bureaucratic nobility was the vast mass
of peasants, three-quarters of the entire population. These
were "the nation" (*narod*), the "dark people" indeed in the
sense of ignorance, but still, as the Russian word for "peasant"
(*krestyanin*) suggests, the Christians par excellence. The special regard, almost awe, in which the peasant masses were held
indicates the strong populist trend in Russian thought. However, there was a chasm between the idealized image and reality. Until 1861, most of the peasants in the Russian Empire
were serfs, the property of noble landlords or (almost as frequently) of the crown. Under Catherine the Great, the peasant
had been little better than a chattel slave, subject to removal
from his ancestral farm, to almost unrestricted sale as property,
and to arbitrary and brutal chastisement. "Emancipation,"
following some minor reforms earlier in the century, amelio-
rated the peasant's position, but still his freedom was restricted
from two directions. The government kept close watch over
his activities through the "land captains." Primary control of
the peasant's movement was left to the village community, or

mir, which, because it was collectively responsible for the tax and redemption payments for the land allotted the peasants at the time of emancipation, would not let its members leave freely. Thus the peasant was subject to the group pressure of his peers as well as to the authority of the government. The power of the *mir* over the individual was by no means a wholly spontaneous development; for centuries, the Czarist regime had in various ways strengthened the *mir* as a convenient instrument of control. But long-established custom also played a vital role.

In many areas of the Russian Empire, the practice of "repartitional tenure" meant that each village commune periodically redistributed its land among the member families. As a result, the individual or the family group had little incentive to undertake long-range improvement of the land. Methods of cultivation tended to be set by custom rather than economic calculation. To a considerable extent, this was the case even in those territories where repartitional tenure did not prevail, for even there the family's allotment of land usually consisted of scattered strips. The size and location of these fragmented holdings required that many of the farming operations be conducted in unison, ordinarily in accordance with long-established patterns. Where new decisions were required, they were made by the *mir* as a collective body in which the less efficient or enterprising members were at least as influential as those who favored modern innovations.

In spite of these circumstances, peasant institutions underwent considerable change in the last years of the Czarist regime. From 1907 on, the government itself fostered these changes in an effort to create a class of "yeomen" farmers attached to the principles of social stability as guarantees for their own property and profits. Measures were envisaged, and to some extent implemented, to break up the *mir,* consolidate the scattered holdings of each peasant family, and thus give fuller scope to the initiative of the individual. There is no doubt that many peasants were eager to become fully independent farmers. By 1917, the less fortunate or less enterprising peasants were beginning to become differentiated in status and attitudes from their more successful brethren, and in some ways this development was accelerated during the confused situation immediately following the revolutions of that year. The more a peasant had, and the more enterprising—and possibly unscrupulous—he was, the more he was apt to receive in the breakup of the nobles' estates. Nevertheless, the peasant whom the Bolsheviks confronted was still deeply immersed in the customary life of his village community.

The Workers

By 1917, the peasants no longer comprised the entire lower stratum. A few million industrial workers gained an inordinately important role in revolutionary activity, both because of their strategic location in the metropolitan centers and railroad junctions and because of the importance ascribed to them by revolutionary doctrine. In the general perspective of pre-Revolutionary history, however, the "proletariat" was relatively insignificant; this was all the more true because the industrial worker was often really a peasant recently, perhaps only temporarily, transplanted to an urban environment.

The Intelligentsia

The rudimentary nature of the middle class was in some ways a more striking difference between pre-Revolutionary Russia and the more advanced Western lands than the lack of individualist farmers, numerous workers, or an independent aristocracy. While the exact relationship between the rise of the European middle classes and the growth of limited, representative government is uncertain, the reciprocal influence of these developments is incontestible. Historically, the middle classes were based on commerce and industry. In the Czarist Empire, however, commercial activities were relatively poorly developed, especially by members of the dominant Russian national group. The post-1890 period saw phenomenal industrial development, exceeding in proportional growth (though not, of course, in absolute increment) that of most of the Western countries. A large part of the industry, however, was controlled by Western investors, and much of the remainder consisted of government enterprises. To the extent to which a Russian commercial and entrepreneurial class had emerged by 1917, it was a new social element, uncertain of its position, relatively unsophisticated, and narrow in its attitudes.

Alongside the businessman, the professional has constituted an essential element of the Western middle class. The usual liberal professions were, of course, represented in the Czarist Empire. Physicians, lawyers, and teachers were numerous and increasingly important. Without the support—economic and psychological—of an independent aristocracy or a self-reliant farmer or business group, however, the professionals tended to become absorbed in the governmental bureaucracy or to spend their lives in frustrating, if altruistic, efforts to improve the lot of the peasantry. Because their professional skills, based on Western experience, provided them with an image of a more rationally organized society, the conditions of Czarist Russia seemed the more repugnant to them. In particular, the illiteracy and high mortality of the peasants appalled the professional groups. Many of those with the most useful skills, such as physicians and teachers (engineers and agricultural technicians, who might have been even more useful in the long run, were scarce and often hardly regarded as professionals), devoted themselves to work in the zemstvo. Others took more revolutionary steps.

Most of the professionals constituted a part of a social group that had no precise Western counterpart, as our very use of the Russian term—intelligentsia—indicates. Generally speaking, membership in the intelligentsia was a matter of self-identification. The highly educated bureaucrat or businessman might or might not regard himself as a member. A half-educated but articulate clerk might aspire to membership. More important than its precise composition was the fact that the intelligentsia, as a comparatively self-conscious and active element, occupied the place between the government and the inarticulate lower classes held by the middle class in Western Europe. The student (including many middle-aged men like Chekhov's "perpetual student"), the scholar, the artist, the professional, tended to constitute the intelligentsia proper. For the most part they were discontented with the situation in the Russian Empire, embarrassed at the "backwardness" of its economic and political development compared to the West (though often simultaneously extolling the inherent superiority of Russian traditions), and ashamed of the oppression and neglect of the peasantry. These attitudes were combined with feelings of frustration over their inability to exert influence on the autocracy, resentment against curbs on intellectual activity, and, often, the bitterness engendered by poverty. Instead of a stabilizing element, the intelligentsia tended to be the spearhead of the forces working for profound disruption of the Czarist order.

THE INTELLECTUAL CLIMATE

The importance of the intelligentsia's dissatisfaction as an element in the climate of opinion favorable to revolution is obvious. But there are other, more subtle ways in which the attitudes of Imperial society seem to have prepared for subsequent developments. The collectivist aspects of the village community hampered individual economic development, and the pressures of conforming to the peer group discouraged independent attitudes. Particularly interesting in this connection is the stress put on unanimous decisions in the rural community. While a considerable measure of discussion took place in village-meetings, where all heads of households were, theoretically at least, equal, a decision by majority vote was unacceptable. Instead, village opinion demanded unanimity in the final decision, even if physical coercion was required to secure the minority's assent.

Pressure for Unanimity

At higher levels of Russian society, the demand for unanimity in the village took the form of pervasive censorship of expression. The most obvious side of this censorship was the official one; with varying scope and effectiveness, the regime sought to suppress ideas hostile to it. In some respects, the "censorship of the Left," however, was more effective and more interesting during the last years of the nineteenth century.* The writer or artist who failed to express the concepts of protest and revolt dominant among the intelligentsia was subjected to a type of unofficial ostracism and criticism few could withstand. While the vectors of official and unofficial pressure represented opposing camps, both failed to honor the inviolability of intellectual freedom.

Rejection of Systematic Rationality

The lack of concern on both Right and Left for fixed principles of civil liberties was characteristic of the fragmentary reception in Russia of Western ideas. The Slavophiles, and some of their successors, explicitly rejected the systematic rationality of Western thought. They argued that one of the great merits of Orthodoxy, in contrast to both Catholicism and Protestantism in the West, was its stress upon mystic

* Its effectiveness declined in the last two decades of Czarist rule.

experience rather than rationalized philosophy. The piety of
the cloister rather than the systems of the scholastics was the
glory of Orthodox monasticism. To some extent, the intellectual attitudes that underlay this position were shared by
the secular intelligentsia. As mentioned earlier, many Russian
intellectuals envied Western rationality. Yet, while German
and French (less often British) philosophers were widely read
in nineteenth- and early twentieth-century Russia, systematic
indigenous philosophy developed only haltingly. Ideas were
plentiful, and frequently highly original; but they served as
spurs to the sentiments and activities of the intelligentsia
rather than as starting points for great integrated systems of
thought.

In a somewhat related fashion, legal principles remained
peripheral to Russian intellectual development. The autocracy
provided a system of courts that, after the 1860's, provided for
juries in criminal cases—sometimes with startling results. However, since the police possessed the administrative right to
exile political offenders, the concept of inviolable rights under
law inherent in Western legal systems did not exist. And it
is notable that in protesting the policies of the regime, the
Russian intelligentsia laid little stress upon establishment of
the rule of law as a safeguard against tyranny.

Intellectual Progress

Again, one should not exaggerate the extent of differences
between Western and Russian intellectual achievement. Legal
scholarship in the last years of the Czarist Empire was impressive, and one might well have expected it to have a strong
impact upon social thinking in the next generation. The rapid
growth of scientific thought in Russia, marked by the emergence of figures of world importance such as the chemist

Dimitry I. Mendeleyev, the psychologist Ivan P. Pavlov, and the mathematician Nikolai I. ,Lobachevsky, indicates the acceptance of a kind of rationality that would inevitably have induced more systematic approaches to general problems of knowledge. The very considerable progress in general education, which promised to reduce illiteracy to modest levels within a generation following the reforms of 1905, might have provided a solid foundation for liberal institutions and social progress.

Messianism

One more aspect of the climate of ideas in the Czarist Empire must be mentioned: the tendency toward messianic conceptions of Russia's role in world history. The Slavophile conviction of the superiority of Orthodoxy in the social and intellectual spheres formed one foundation for this view. The Slavophiles' more militant successors, the Panslavs, envisaged a secular mission for the Russian nation—that of uniting all the Slavic peoples, assuming a dominant position in Europe, and reforming the "decadent" West. Except for brief intervals, such radically ethnocentric and expansionist ideas had little influence on official foreign policy. The concept of the civilizing mission of Russia—not basically different from the theories influencing contemporary West European imperialism—was more important. By the end of the nineteenth century, the Russian Empire embraced over 166 million inhabitants in an area of 8 million square miles. Over half of the population was non-Russian. True, many of the remainder were East Slavs, closely related to the Russians, and most of the others were Europeans living in the border areas. The greatest expansion of the Empire had taken place in Asia, however, and there the Czarist proconsuls believed that they were entitled to impose the benefits of Russian culture and material progress.

The Absence of Racist Attitudes

It should be pointed out that the Russians, on the whole, did not share the rigid attitudes of racial superiority and segregation that characterized many West European colonizers. Unlike the West European colonial empires, separated by thousands of miles of ocean from their home countries and inhabited by peoples whose physical characteristics differentiated them from the Europeans, the Russian Empire stretched in an unbroken mass across Eurasia. To a considerable degree, the physical characteristics of the Empire's population represented a series of gradual changes from the blond, semi-"Nordic" types of the Baltic coast to the darker, flatter Mongol features of the Altai. Then, too, in contrast to the dramatic "expansion of Western Europe" in the sixteenth century, Russian contact with non-Europeans had lasted for more than a millennium, involving relationships of subjection as well as ascendancy. Some observers would also ascribe part of the differences in Russian racial attitudes to Orthodox influence, especially as contrasted to northwest European Calvinism. But whatever the reasons, this aspect of Russian heritage—the combination of strong national pride, to the point of a messianic complex, and a relatively tolerant attitude toward racial differences—has exerted an important influence on more recent Soviet contacts with the non-European world.

THE REVOLUTION AND AFTER

It would be fascinating to trace both the constant and the changing aspects of Russian thought and practice under the impact of revolution. Here, however, we can only note the most essential facts of Soviet history; brief as it is, this summary should provide the reader with a sense of chronological development.

The first revolution of 1917, in March, was quite unplanned. Under the terrible strain of World War I, the rigid and inefficient structure of the Czarist regime broke down. For a few months, liberals and moderates imbued with Western concepts of governmental and social order maintained a precarious grip on the central authority. In November, they were swept away, almost without bloodshed, by the Bolshevik Revolution. A few thousand determined revolutionists, guided by the ideological and organizational theories that we shall examine in the next chapter, inherited the place of the Czarist bureaucracy. Among the main reasons for their success was their willingness to promise immediate distribution of land to the peasants (with covert reservations concerning the more distant future) and immediate peace negotiations with Germany.

Within a few months, however, the Bolsheviks were engaged in a desperate struggle against a variety of domestic "counter-revolutionary" movements, which were sporadically and ineffectively supported by the Central Powers and the Western Allies. By 1920, the Bolsheviks had triumphed fully, except in some outlying areas of the former Empire, but they did so at a terrible cost. Millions had died in battle or as a result of famine, and the relatively small industrial and transportation capital of the country had been largely dissipated. A large part of the old nobility, intelligentsia, and bureaucracy had fled or died. These catastrophic events made it easier for the Bolsheviks to carry out the remodeling of Russian society, for much of the old social fabric had disintegrated. In the early 1920's, their most urgent need, however, was to ensure a minimal livelihood for the surviving population and to maintain a modicum of national strength. The long period of the "New Economic Policy" (1921–28) was essentially a holding operation in which the Bolshevik leadership sought time to prepare for the next stage.

Stalin

At the beginning of this period, Lenin, a truly charismatic figure, became incapacitated (he died in early 1924), and leadership was gradually assumed by one of his less prominent lieutenants, Joseph V. Stalin. In a series of crafty and ruthless maneuvers, Stalin defeated and discredited his rivals in the Communist Party (as the Bolshevik group called itself after March, 1918). By 1928, Stalin ruled supreme. He then launched a crash program of industrialization, the so-called Five-Year Plans. Simultaneously, he carried out the collectivization of agriculture, forcing the individual peasant-farmers into large kolkhozes (collective farms). Collectivization was achieved at the cost of several million lives and a catastrophic drop in food production; as we shall see, its results are still by no means certain. It did, however, give the Soviet regime complete physical control of the countryside. The more clear-cut successes of the Five-Year Plans greatly increased the industrial basis for Soviet military power. In the period between 1934 and 1938, Stalin consolidated his absolute dictatorship by a vast blood purge of the Communist Party, which brought in its wake the destruction of most of the old Bolshevik leadership.

The Crisis of World War II

Scarcely had this crisis passed before the U.S.S.R. was involved in World War II, first as a quasi-ally of the Axis powers, then (when Hitler turned on the U.S.S.R.) as a member of the anti-Axis coalition. The war, which at one point saw Hitler's forces occupying territory that had sheltered more than one-third of the Soviet population, wrought enormous destruction. The Soviet death toll—in the neighborhood of 20 million—was greater than that of any other belligerent, even the defeated powers, and the per-capita death rate higher than that of any other country with the possible exception of Poland and Yugoslavia. Economic losses were also enormous, though the amazing success of Soviet evacuation and rebuilding of industry in the Urals and other regions prevented complete economic collapse. The Nazi invasion revealed that a large proportion of the Soviet population was so alienated from its own government that it welcomed foreign "deliverance." But the cruel policies of the Nazis, combined with the strength of the Communist apparatus and residual Russian patriotism, enabled the Soviet regime to maintain enough popular support to win. It may, perhaps, never be possible to estimate the exact measure in which each member of the anti-Axis coalition contributed to the final victory; but unquestionably, the U.S.S.R.'s contribution was enormous. Consequently, and also as a result of Germany's and Japan's elimination, the prestige of the Communist regime greatly increased, though (as Stalin privately admitted) its material strength had been sapped. The Soviet rulers have since taken advantage of this circumstance to claim that the superiority of the Soviet system has been proved in the test of war.

Stalin's Successors

For seven and one-half years after the end of World War II, Stalin retained his undisputed dictatorial powers. While the U.S.S.R. rebuilt its physical plant, Stalin rigidly maintained barriers to intercourse between the Soviet population and the outside world. His death, in March, 1953, unleashed a period of sharp struggle between his lieutenants, culminating in Nikita Khrushchev's victory, in January, 1955. In October, 1964, Khrushchev was, in turn, replaced by a "collective leadership" in which no one man appears to dominate.

SUGGESTED READING · CHAPTER 1

The following general histories of Russia are valuable:

CHARQUES, R. D. *A Short History of Russia.* New York: E. P. Dutton & Company; Everyman paperback, 1956.

CLARKSON, JESSE D. *A History of Russia.* New York: Random House, 1961.

ELLISON, HERBERT J. *History of Russia.* New York: Holt, Rinehart, & Winston, 1964.

FLORINSKY, MICHAEL T. *Russia: A History and an Interpretation.* 2 vols. New York: The Macmillan Company, 1953.

MAZOUR, ANATOLE. *Russia, Past and Present.* Princeton, N.J.: D. Van Nostrand Co., 1951.

PARES, BERNARD. *A History of Russia.* New York: Alfred A. Knopf, 1953.

RIASANOVSKY, NICHOLAS. *A History of Russia.* London and New York: Oxford University Press, 1963.

SUMNER, B. H. *A Short History of Russia.* New York: Harcourt, Brace and Company, 1949; Harvest paperback, 1962.

VERNADSKY, GEORGE. *A History of Russia.* New Haven, Conn.: Yale University Press, 1954.

Very competent surveys of the Soviet period of Russian history and its immediate background of revolutionary ferment are:

TREADGOLD, DONALD W. *Twentieth Century Russia.* Chicago: Rand McNally & Company, 1964.

VON RAUCH, GEORG. *A History of Soviet Russia.* 5th rev. ed. New York: Frederick A. Praeger, 1967.

Those deeply interested in the Bolshevik Revolution and its immediate aftermath should read:

CARR, EDWARD HALLETT. *A History of Soviet Russia.* 6 vols. New York: The Macmillan Company, 1950–64.

CHAMBERLIN, WILLIAM HENRY. *The Russian Revolution.* 2 vols. New York: The Macmillan Company, 1960.

SCHAPIRO, LEONARD. *The Origin of the Communist Autocracy.* Cambridge, Mass.: Harvard University Press, 1955; New York: Praeger paperback, 1965.

WOLFE, BERTRAM. *Three Who Made a Revolution.* New York: The Dial Press, 1948; Boston: Beacon Press paperback, 1955.

More specialized works on earlier Russian history of particular interest are:

BLACK, CYRIL E. (ed.). *The Transformation of Russian Society.* Cambridge, Mass.: Harvard University Press, 1960. An impressive collaborative effort to compare pre-Revolutionary and Soviet society.

KORNILOV, A. A. *Modern Russian History.* New York: Alfred A. Knopf, 1943. A brilliant treatment of eighteenth- and nineteenth-century Russia by a nineteenth-century Russian historian.

MASARYK, THOMAS G. *The Spirit of Russia.* 2 vols. New York: The Macmillan Company, 1955. A penetrating analysis of Russian thought in the nineteenth century by a great Czechoslovakian statesman.

MAVOR, JAMES. *An Economic History of Russia.* 2 vols. New York: E. P. Dutton & Company, 1914. The only comprehensive treatment of economic development under the Czars.

MAYNARD, JOHN. *Russia in Flux.* New York: The Macmillan Company, 1947. A controversial but stimulating interpretation of the main currents of Russian history.

PETROVICH, MICHAEL B. *The Emergence of Russian Panslavism, 1856–1870.* New York: Columbia University Press, 1956. A penetrating study of a crucial period in the development of Russian ideology.

PIPES, RICHARD (ed.). *The Russian Intelligentsia.* New York: Columbia University Press, 1961. An important collection of essays on the situation of the intelligentsia under the Czarist regime and the Soviet system.

ROBINSON, GEROID T. *Rural Russia under the Old Regime.* New York: The Macmillan Company, 1949. A masterful description of the peasant base of old Russia.

WALLACE, DONALD MACKENZIE. *Russia.* New York: Henry Holt and Company, 1905. In spite of its early date, this work has remained unsurpassed for its insight into Russian social conditions.

2

THE IDEOLOGY

In all societies, political culture is an amalgam of traditional, often subconscious, influences, and deliberate indoctrination by dominant institutions. In *The American Dilemma*, Gunnar Myrdal was able to identify an "American Creed," which included those democratic principles inculcated by the schools, the churches, the mass media, and other institutions, as well as those traditions transmitted from generation to generation. Similar political-cultural (deliberate-traditional) amalgams have been detected in most other modern societies. As we have seen, the traditional element is strong in the U.S.S.R., too. What distinguishes the Soviet political system is the near monopoly over the means of overt inculcation of political culture that is held by a single institutional complex, which we may call the "regime." The Soviet regime claims to exercise its monopoly in favor of a single body of ideas, the Communist ideology. Using this ideology, the regime seeks not merely to influence a limited range of political behavior but to remake the entire society. In order to carry out this totalitarian transformation, a new human personality must, according to the ideology, develop. Moreover, the ideology claims to be a systematic, indeed a scientific, doctrine capable of guiding the process of human transformation. An examination of this supposed scientific approach to social problems is the prerequisite to understanding the present Soviet system. For, whether or not the regime has followed its purported blueprint, a doctrine given such intense overt allegiance must, inevitably, exert a strong psychological influence.

THEORETICAL FOUNDATIONS

Officially, the body of Communist ideology is called "Marxism-Leninism."* As the name indicates, the ideology is not an indigenous Russian growth, for Karl Marx and his collaborator, Friedrich Engels, were German by birth. Their works and Lenin's constitute the "classics" of present-day Soviet ideology. Although Lenin built upon the basic Marxist structure, he modified it in many respects—rarely admitting that he had done so, however. His successors have introduced additional modifications, but "Leninism," to a much greater extent than "Marxism," remains the foundation of Soviet ideological thinking. Indeed, several of the most far-reaching modifications of Leninism made by Lenin's immediate successor, the Georgian Stalin, have been disavowed or allowed to fall into disuse. This circumstance is important, not least because it represents a return to the peculiarly Russian aspect of Communism. For Lenin (though of mixed ethnic descent) was Russian to the core, and many of the changes he introduced in Marx's doctrine reflect the influence of the Russian heritage. The return to Lenin promoted by Nikita Khrushchev and his successors (almost all of whom are Russians) bears the stamp of an earthy Russian mentality. Still, it may be argued, these national influences are secondary; for, through all changes, Marx's aim —the creation of the "new man"—has remained.

Materialism

Materialism, probably the most fundamental premise of the doctrine, has also remained essentially unchanged since Marx. According to Marxism-Leninism, all being is determined by

---

* This chapter draws heavily upon Communist terminology. Its connotation to the Western reader is often quite different from the real meaning of the terms—sometimes designedly so, for Communists are skilled in using words to convey one meaning to the unaware outsider, another to the initiated. To avoid misunderstanding, such terms will be enclosed in quotation marks when first used, and their implications explained.

the nature of the material "base." The situation of mankind is said to depend upon the "relationships of production." In each epoch of human history, given types of tools (using the term in a broad sense) are available, and human labor utilizes them in a certain way. The nature of this relation of man to his tools requires a special form of social organization—"the relationship of production," or "base." All other aspects of human society—family relations, religion, government, law, art, philosophy, literature—are included in the "superstructure." The elements of the superstructure are mere reflections of the base and change in their nature as man's organized relationship to his tools changes.

Expressed in these simple terms (avoiding the numerous complications and qualifications that Soviet and non-Soviet Marxists have discussed), materialism seems either self-evident or absurd, depending on the philosophical premises of the observer. Accepted implicitly by the Soviet Communist (and apparently by most educated Soviet citizens outside the Party), however, materialism has tremendous psychological implications. The world, all of human existence, is "explained" without reference to God. Consequently, Marxism-Leninism has always been rigorously atheistic, not merely agnostic. No religious influence can encroach (so long as the doctrine is accepted) upon the Communist's loyalty to the ideology and its spokesmen. The world, in both its physical and its human aspects, is explained "scientifically." As a result, the discoveries of the natural sciences receive enormous emphasis in the U.S.S.R. Except in more or less isolated cases—when it seems to conflict with Leninist principles or with the personal interests of a leader of the regime—scientific investigation receives great support. It seems probable, however, that materialism itself (as well as practical necessity) encourages emphasis upon the more immediate aspects of scientific work—those permitting immediate technical application—rather than upon the more abstract elements of scientific thought. Thus, the stress in Soviet activity and publicity is upon the conquest of nature, whether by Sputnik or polar exploration, rather than, for example, on the theory of relativity. Basic theory is often accepted ready-made from foreign sources.

Dialectic

The striking and readily comprehended successes of Soviet science and technology in conquering nature have unquestionably deepened popular confidence in the ability of science to explain and accomplish everything. In turn, this confidence strengthens the ideological teaching of materialism. To many foreign observers it has seemed that the young Soviet-trained citizens are indeed attached to a materialism based principally, if not exclusively, upon the kind of natural scientific materialism known (though not dominant) in the West for two centuries. To the official Communist ideologist, such a view is anathema, for by omitting the second basic aspect of Marxist-Leninist doctrine, the "dialectic," it reduces the system to "vulgar materialism." According to Marx (whom Lenin ostensibly fully accepted on this count), "dialectical materialism" is an indivisible whole. Unfortunately, the dialectic aspects of the doctrine are very difficult to explain concisely—and indeed there appears to be considerable confusion among its adherents (including Marx) in the explanation of this theory. Its fundamental aspect is the simultaneous presence, in all phases of being, of contradictory elements—"thesis" and "antithesis." The interaction of the contradictory elements leads to change—the formation of a new state ("synthesis"), which, however, also contains contradictory elements that will eventually result in change. Marx wisely refrained from applying this recondite concept to the world of nature. His disciple Engels was less cautious; for example, he maintained that the change of water when heat is withdrawn represented a dialectic

transformation to—ice! Lenin and subsequent Soviet Marxists
have followed this interpretation, which to most outside observers appears to be a meaningless and absurd play on words.
For example, the present author saw a Soviet dissertation in
which the student asserted that a chemist, after studying
Marxism-Leninism, was able to show how the change of
amino acid to albumen represented the dialectic formation of
a new synthesis.

A major aspect of the dialectic transformation is the "transformation of quantity to quality." According to this principle,
minor, imperceptible changes (in "quantity") occur in a sub-
stance or state without altering its nature, or "quality." When
the accumulation of minor changes reaches a certain point,
however, the change of "quality" occurs all at once—the "dialectic leap." This "leap," according to all the "classics," up to
and including Lenin, is always sudden—as the example of
change of water to ice was intended to demonstrate. This explanation probably contains a clue to why Communist theorists are attracted to the dialectic explanation, for it provides a
ready justification for revolution. Therefore, Stalin, who was
bent upon the consolidation of his dictatorship, feared the
"explosive" leap and revised Marxism-Leninism to maintain
that dialectic change under some conditions was gradual.

Indeed, it appeared that toward the end of his life, Stalin
was moving in the direction of rejecting much of dialectic
theory. In 1951, he referred (in "Marxism and Problems of
Linguistics") to the "chaos" that would be introduced into human life if language changed when relationships of production
changed. He declared that certain elements of human activity, e.g., language, logic, and, apparently, the natural sciences,
stood outside the framework of dialectical development in
history. Since Stalin's death, the return to Leninism has cast
doubt upon these alterations, which, whatever Stalin's motivation, tended to bring Soviet thought somewhat closer to

Western ideas. Today, "dialectic logic" is once again opposed to "formal logic," though adherents of the latter have not been silenced.

Historical Materialism

The practical importance of the dialectic to Soviet Communism has, however, lain in its relation to the historical development of society rather than in its questionable philosophical validity or in its dubious application to the natural sciences. "Historical materialism," that is, the application of the dialectic to history, supposedly offers the only valid explanation of social development. However doubtful this assertion may be, Marx's original stress upon dialectic development did have the virtue of focusing attention on those elements of change and interrelation of social phenomena that many of his contemporaries and immediate predecessors had neglected. As noted in the discussion of materialism, Marx contended that every stage of history has been marked by divisions of human society corresponding to man's relationship to tools. As the tools change, the relationships change; hence the existing social order becomes unstable as the contradictory elements within it emerge. More specifically, a new dominant class rises to replace the old; at the appropriate time, the new class seizes power by revolution, usually violent. Thus, the feudal nobility replaced the slaveowners of antiquity, and "capitalist" entrepreneurs (the "bourgeoisie") replaced the nobility.

Obviously, the Marxist was really interested in the next stage—the replacement of the bourgeoisie by the industrial workers, or "proletariat," for this final change would usher in the era of the "classless" society, in which man would move toward perfection without further recourse to violent revolutions. From the philosophical standpoint, the insistence on the motivating force of class conflict throughout all previous human history, to be superseded at an arbitrary time by harmonious progress, seems untenable. Psychologically, however, the explanation has its appeal. It accepts, in part, the hard-headed skepticism of the cyclical theories of history—each stage of human society develops, unfolds its maximum possibilities, and then declines, to be replaced by a new cycle of human development. The Marxist type of cyclical development, however, avoids ultimate pessimism by the reassurance that, in terms of human progress, each cycle is higher than the preceding one. Moreover, each cycle constitutes a prerequisite for a still more progressive cycle. Finally, a stage (close at hand) is reached in which the necessity for the violent replacement of an outworn social structure ends, and the type of unilateral progress espoused by the eighteenth-century utopians appears. In considerable measure, then, Marxism-Leninism has appealed to both optimists and skeptics; its avowed contempt for "utopias" is coupled to a promise of perfection in this world.

Imperialism

Still, the emphasis of the ideology is upon the transformation from "capitalism" to "socialism." Prior to Lenin, this transformation was predicted for an advanced industrial country in which the workers constitute the overwhelming majority of the population. Marx developed immensely elaborate arguments to show that all value was produced by the workers, but that the capitalists systematically appropriated the "surplus value," i.e., all above that which the workers need to reproduce their kind. The argument appears to have little factual validity or even systematic relation to the rest of historical materialism, but its appeal for workers who are really destitute has been enormous. In the early part of this century, however, Lenin was confronted with the necessity of explaining why workers in many West European countries were not becoming progressively more impoverished, but, on the contrary, were making economic strides. His answer was the theory of "imperialism, the highest stage of capitalism." The essence of his argument was that the immensely concentrated capitalist monopolies in advanced industrial countries could afford to bribe their proletariats to assist the capitalists in "exporting exploitation" to less developed areas where (one could deduce from Marxist theory) capital returns would be higher. Thus, improvement of the condition of a minority of the workers (West European whites) was achieved at the expense of a huge majority of workers and peasants (largely colored) in colonial and semi-colonial countries.

The Weakest Link

In retrospect, Lenin appears to have been uncannily foresighted in advancing a theory of imperialism so well adapted to present Communist appeals to the underdeveloped nations. At the time, however, he was more concerned with the course to be taken by the proletariat of Western Europe and, above all, with the immediate future of revolution in Russia. It is true that Lenin hesitated for a long time before definitely asserting that a "socialist" revolution could occur in so backward a country as Russia, but he maintained, at an early date, that a "bourgeois" revolution in Russia could ignite "proletarian" revolutions throughout Europe. According to Lenin's theory of the "weakest link," revolution would not occur first in the more advanced industrial countries, where the workers were temporarily bought off by minor concessions, but in a country that was in the initial and more painful stages of industrialization. Such a country's capitalists, though in an early stage of development, had to compete with those of more advanced countries in securing colonies and spheres of influence. To do so, the capitalists (like those in heavily industrialized countries) used the state machinery, the government of their country, as an instrument. As the competition among the capitalist-controlled governments became more severe, it was attended by international friction, armaments races, and, eventually, war—World War I. These developments imposed terrible burdens upon the working classes of all the competing and warring nations. These burdens were most severe, to the point of being unendurable, upon the small, weak proletariat and the larger, inarticulate peasantry of the country that was only in the initial stage of industrialization, but that was fully engaged in the unequal imperialist contest. This country was, of course, Russia; and the theory justified what Lenin was really most interested in asserting—that Russia was ripe for revolution.

THE DIRECTIVES

Russia was ripe for _a_ revolution, but not yet inevitably drawn to _proletarian_ revolution. For Lenin, as for Marx, the strongly deterministic theory of historical materialism was accompanied by an insistence (which many critics have felt to be philosophically inconsistent) upon the need for conscious, deliberate human action to speed and smooth the course of social development. Both Marx and Lenin maintained that theory and action are inseparable, but Lenin's emphasis on organizing a revolution was much stronger than Marx's. Indeed, many students of Lenin's work have felt that he was primarily interested in social engineering rather than in social theory.

The Party

To carry out the proletarian revolution, according to Lenin, a highly organized party was necessary. Without the leadership of this "vanguard of the proletariat," the working class, he said, lacked consciousness of its own true interests, to say nothing of the ability to implement them. This party (which of course turned out to be the Bolsheviks, Lenin's own faction of the Russian Social Democratic Workers Party) should embrace all the "conscious" elements of the proletariat and persons of other classes (like Lenin himself) who adhered to the proletarian cause. All members, Lenin held, must actively participate in the party's work, which, under the conditions of the Czarist regime, had to be illegal, therefore conspiratorial. But even where the party was legal (as was briefly the case in Russia), it must retain a conspiratorial substratum. In order to bring about the revolution, all means are legitimate: "Morality is that which serves to destroy the old exploiting society and to unite all toilers around the proletariat."*

Democratic Centralism

The guiding organizational principle of the party was "democratic centralism." According to Lenin, this concept meant choosing leaders (in a pyramidal system of indirect election) by the rank and file, followed by binding decisions from above. Between elections, the party leaders were supreme, and any effort to agitate or combine against their decisions was treason to the party. Similarly, party policies might be debated openly (in the appropriate party meetings or committees) before decisions were made; after that no opposition was permitted. How "democratic centralism," still nominally the guiding organizational principle of the Communist Party of the Soviet Union, works in practice we shall consider in the next chapter. Let us simply note here that, in pre-Revolutionary times, debates and elections could not take place with any regularity in the underground party. Hence, democratic centralism meant, in practice, Lenin's continued domination. Even after the Revolution, however, he usually avoided the naked application of force within the party to accomplish his purposes.

* *Sochineniya* (Leningrad: Partizdat, 1935), XXV, 392.

Revolution

In his last years, Marx had considered the possibility of a peaceful victory of the proletariat. He held that in countries where elections and representative government had some meaning (specifically in Great Britain and the United States) the workers' parties might secure power by winning control of the legislative bodies. Ultimately, Lenin rejected this possibility:

> It [the capitalist state] cannot be replaced by the proletarian State (the dictatorship of the proletariat) through mere "withering away," but, in accordance with the general rule, can only be brought about by a violent revolution.*

Lenin did, however, envisage one exception:

> One cannot deny that in individual cases, as exceptions, for example in some small state, it is *possible* that after the victory of the social revolution in a large neighboring state the bourgeoisie would peacefully give up its power if it became convinced of the hopelessness of resistance and preferred to save their heads.†

For decades, Lenin's dicta on the necessity of violent revolution were not questioned by Soviet leaders (though often tacitly ignored, for diplomatic reasons). In 1956, however, Nikita Khrushchev and other Soviet spokesmen referred to the possibility of a "parliamentary path to socialism." They denied that this constituted a contradiction of Lenin, and referred somewhat vaguely to exceptions he had envisaged. Apparently, the exception the latter-day Soviet leaders really had in mind was the "small country" Lenin referred to (again with considerable prescience) in the passage just quoted. Specifically, Soviet spokesmen alluded to the "peaceful" Communist takeover in Czechoslovakia, in 1948. This coup had indeed been

---

* *State and Revolution* (New York: Vanguard Press, 1929), p. 128.
† *Sochineniya* (4th ed.; Moscow: Gosudarstvennoe Izdatelstvo Politicheskoi Literatury, 1949), XXIII, 57.

accomplished without much bloodshed; but it was brought off by mass demonstrations, hoodlumism, the threat of unchecked violence by Communists within the country, and the veiled hint of intervention by overwhelming Soviet forces strategically deployed on almost all of the Czechoslovak frontiers.

In contrast to the monolithic rigidity demanded by Stalin, recent Communist practice has granted the satellite regimes a certain degree of flexibility in conduct of local affairs. But all orthodox Communists agree that, however the "workers' party" comes to power, it must establish a "dictatorship of the proletariat." The purpose of the dictatorship is to suppress the exploiting classes (bourgeoisie and remnants of the nobility) and prepare the way for "socialism." Socialism, in its turn, is (according to Marx, Lenin, and their Soviet successors) a necessary transitional stage to true "Communism." Under socialism, the means of production are placed in the hands of the workers' state; private enterprise in commerce, manufacturing, or farming is eliminated as quickly as feasible. Legal and social controls remain necessary, however, not only to suppress remnants of the exploiting classes, but to ensure proper work and social behavior on the part of workers and peasants who still are influenced by "remnants of bourgeois mentality." The principle of socialism must be "from each according to his ability, to each according to his work."

Socialism in One Country

Both Marx and Lenin had thought that the stage at which compulsion is still necessary would be brief. To Marx, the great economic machine built by capitalism, once in the hands of the workers, would be almost able to furnish the abundance of goods required by the formula of true Communism—"from each according to his ability, to each according to his needs." Lenin realized that such abundance would not be achieved for many years by the backward Russian economy, but he believed that the revolution, once started, would, via chain reaction (to use an anachronistic analogy), spread to the more industrialized countries. Then the workers' governments of these countries, coming to the rescue of the Russian socialist state, which had shown them the way, would aid Russia to build up its economy rapidly. Lenin never gave up this hope, but, being practical, he concentrated in his last years upon strengthening the proletarian dictatorship achieved in Russia. This was the beginning of the practice of "socialism in one country," which Stalin elevated to the level of theory. To develop the Russian economy rapidly without outside aid, a Spartan regime of material privation was required, resembling the early period of capitalism with its harsh conditions of labor, long hours, and bare subsistence wages. Indeed, one Bolshevik economist explicitly avowed the necessity of a period of "the primitive accumulation of capital under socialism" at the expense of the mass of the population. Though Stalin never officially accepted the theory of "primitive accumulation," it seems to have been his real guide in the frightful deprivations occasioned by the collectivization of agriculture and the industrialization of the early Five-Year Plans (1928–41). Soviet leaders assert today that the U.S.S.R. has reached a stage where economic progress is compatible with the provision of considerable consumers' goods. But the "primitive accumulation" theory in fact, though not in name, is still the Communist prescription for underdeveloped countries.

The Omnipotent State

Many Marxists (even in the U.S.S.R.) had anticipated that, as socialism developed, the state and its repressive organs would gradually diminish in scope. Stalin, however, sharply denied this contention:

> We stand for the withering away of the state. At the same time we stand for strengthening of the dictatorship of the proletariat,

which is the mightiest and strongest state power that has ever existed. The highest development of state power with the object of preparing the conditions *for* the withering away of state power —that is the Marxist formula. Is it contradictory? Yes, it is "contradictory." But this contradiction is bound up with life, and it fully reflects Marx's dialectics.*

This passage suggests the psychological utility of the concept of the dialectic, however dubious its theoretical relevance may have been. In practice, the emphasis on the increased power of the state meant not only forced industrialization and collectivization, but the maintenance of a vast military establishment and a ubiquitous police. In fact, Stalin, in the 1930's, placed greater stress upon the need for defending the Soviet Union (increasingly identified in his speeches with the Russian nation) than upon preparing the economic basis for Communism. After 1933, the rise of Nazi power in Germany provided more than adequate reason for this emphasis. The view of the Soviet state as the "fortress of revolution" in a hostile "capitalist encirclement" long predated any major threat from what the Communists described generically as "fascist" regimes, however. Even in Lenin's day, foreign Communist parties had been obliged to subordinate their immediate interests to the aim of building up Soviet strength. Under Stalin, this process was carried to extreme lengths. At the same time, he contended that the successes of socialism in the U.S.S.R. made both its foreign and domestic enemies (the "remnants of the exploiting classes" and those controlled by "bourgeois mentality") more desperate in their efforts to overthrow the Soviet regime. This theory was the doctrinal justification for the Great Purge of the 1930's and the maintenance of arbitrary and ruthless police controls. After Stalin's death, the theory of the increasing antagonism of internal enemies was

* Joseph V. Stalin, *Works* (Moscow: Foreign Languages Publishing House, 1955), XII, 381.

officially repudiated, doubtless because it was recognized as a
weapon more readily turned against the Communist Party itself than against the Party's real enemies.

Transition to Communism

The role of the state is very intimately related to the transition to full Communism, the ultimate goal of all Marxists.
While stressing this goal, Marx himself was wise enough to
avoid setting a precise schedule for its attainment or defining
its characteristics. Both Lenin and Stalin were equally cautious. In 1961, however, when Khrushchev was at the height
of his power, the Soviet Communist Party adopted a new program declaring that the U.S.S.R. was making the transition
toward full Communism. The "material and technical basis,"
the program declared, would be completed by 1980. By that
time, two basic prerequisites were to "come close" to being
attained: the provision of goods "to each according to his
needs"; and the establishment of a single system of public
ownership of the means of production in contrast to the present division between "socialist" (state-owned) and "coopera-
tive" property. Discussion in the Soviet press following the
program adoption was more concrete. Clearly, "to each according to his needs" could not entail the satisfaction of unlimited
desires. Material production would be fully adequate, Soviet
spokesmen said, to supply real necessities. Gradually, more
needs (medical services and education are already free) would
be satisfied by free distribution, in place of the present money-
exchange system. Among the goods to be distributed free of
charge by 1980 were listed noon lunches, local transportation,
and housing (including heat and utilities). Money wages would
gradually be leveled, although wage differentials would remain at least until 1980.

The elimination of money incentives is regarded as an essential aspect of the achievement of full Communism, for each

must work "according to his ability" without regard to material reward. The regime's ideologues recognize that attainment of this goal, as well as voluntary limitation of consumption to what is really needed, requires a radical transformation of human psychology. The "new Communist man" must be created. The observance of the rules of "Communist conduct" must become "an organic need and habit." A major change must be the elimination of the differences between manual and intellectual labor. At present, Soviet society officially contains two classes "of toilers"—the industrial workers and the peasants, and a "stratum" of intellectuals and white-collar workers. Full Communism, on the other hand, must be "classless." Ultimately, even national distinctions (especially language) must be effaced, but the Party program recognized that this process would take much longer than the elimination of classes. As less and less time is spent on material production, the individual, it is said, will have greater freedom to develop his talents. His leisure will be beneficially employed for his own cultural, intellectual, and physical development; for sports and artistic endeavor; and for public service.

The transition to Communism described in the 1961 Party program is still a part of the official ideology. In the last three years, however, fewer and fewer references to the program have been made. The resolutions of the 1966 Party Congress are now treated as a new "program"; while these resolutions refer to the ultimate attainment of Communism, they neither discuss the matter in detail nor set a date for the realization of this goal. It seems highly probable that the present Soviet leadership is now aware that the material abundance Communism presupposes is not likely to be reached by 1980. Lacking a prospect of material abundance, the regime cannot hope to introduce the principle "to each according to his needs," but must retain material rewards for an indefinite period.

Several policy developments seem to point in this direction.

Of late, there has been little or no emphasis on wage-leveling. Instead, Soviet citizens have been encouraged to use their earnings to acquire "personal" property. (Personal property, as distinguished from "private" property, is not used to produce "unearned income.") One such instance: Rather than moving toward "free" provision of housing for all, the system is encouraging individuals to provide for their own housing needs. When Khrushchev was in power, individual home construction was discouraged; today, both individual and co-operative construction are considered essential—they provide one-third of all urban housing—and are highly praised. Again, three years ago, private gardening by farmers was discouraged (see Chapter 7); it is now treated as a laudable initiative. Finally, on a more general level, the 1961 program assumed that "social measures" would replace "legal coercion" (see Chapter 6), but most of these social measures have since fallen into disuse.

The apparent retreat from the drive toward full Communism is related to a change in the regime's perception of world conditions. Even the 1961 program recognized that, by 1980, only the "basis" for full Communism will have been laid; as the program noted, until a "developed Communist society" is achieved and "the final settlement of the contradictions between capitalism and Communism in the world arena in favor of Communism" takes place, the Soviet state cannot wither away. Khrushchev had optimistically acclaimed "the shining image of a [Communist] Party that is marching forward victoriously throughout the whole world." But, since 1961, the Soviet leadership has come to realize that the final settlement with capitalism is a distant prospect. The determination exhibited by the United States and its allies during the 1962 Cuban missile confrontation and in subsequent crises, plus the recovery of the U.S. economic growth rate to levels about equal to those of the U.S.S.R., has demonstrated that capitalism is far from collapse. A recent Soviet article foresaw a very protracted period of capitalist influences that would hinder the development of the "new Soviet man":

> All of this ["petty bourgeois love of abundance in material goods and pleasure"] has already become the scourge of capitalist society in the West, and from there the tendencies reach us. The power of things will doubtless become a serious problem in the raising of new generations.*

The 1961 program had also insisted that while the U.S.S.R. was "opening the new road" to Communism, it would have to facilitate the advance of other states of the "socialist camp" in order that they could all achieve full Communism "more or less simultaneously in the same historical epoch." But, even under the most favorable conditions, it would be enormously difficult to provide hundreds of millions of impoverished Chinese with the material abundance the Soviet regime considers a prerequisite for Communism. Apparently, the inept policies of the Peking Communist regime have restricted China's limited potential for economic advance. The bitter controversies between the Soviet and Chinese regimes have made it impossible for the U.S.S.R. to play an effective role in preparing China for Communism and have, perhaps, caused the Soviet leaders to wonder whether it is really desirable for the Chinese Communists to achieve a powerful economy.

Marxism-Leninism—A Science

To the outside observer, the developments just described would seem to provide the Soviet leadership with ample reason to stretch out or abandon the timetable for achieving Communism. From their standpoint, the matter is not so simple. Obviously, the Soviet citizens who suffered terribly for decades and, more recently, endured considerable deprivation in order

* I. Yefremov in *Komsomolskaya Pravda*, January 28, 1966, as translated in *Current Digest of the Soviet Press*, XVIII, No. 6, 17.

to move toward Communism will be disheartened if the regime reneges on the definite promise of the 1961 program: "The Party solemnly proclaims: The present generation of Soviet people shall live under Communism."

But, eliminating the timetable for attaining Communism would not merely cost the regime popularity. Communist ideology has always insisted that Communism is not just a highly desirable goal that one should strive to attain but a historical development that can be scientifically predicted. According to the ideology, Marxism-Leninism is just as scientific in its analysis of social development as are the natural sciences. Again, to the outside observer, historical materialism exhibits little if any ability to predict—a major attribute of true science. Marx predicted the increasing impoverishment of the proletariat in the industrialized countries; the opposite came to pass. Lenin adapted the original theory by adding the new concept of imperialism. Lenin himself, regarding imperialism as the last stage of capitalism, predicted imminent world revolution. When, instead, dictatorships like Nazism arose, Communist ideologues declared that these "fascist" regimes represented capitalism's final attempt to stave off revolution. Obviously, any theory can be "preserved" if it is altered whenever factual developments contradict it. But such a theory has neither predictive utility nor scientific value.

Occasionally, the spokesmen of Soviet Communism admit past ideological errors. Stalin, in 1941, "corrected" Engels' derogatory evaluation of the role of the Russian commander Mikhail I. Kutuzov in the Napoleonic wars. Two decades later, Khrushchev told a Romanian audience that Lenin's views on the inevitability of war were subject to revision. The reversal of a tenet advanced by Stalin (who has, in fact, been dropped as a "classic") was noted above. Ordinarily, however, Soviet Communist statements stress the continuity and consistency of Marxist-Leninist doctrine. This emphasis, instilled by an unchallenged system of indoctrination, has tended to strengthen the Soviet citizens' belief that Marxism-Leninism provides not only a sure guide to social development but an absolute assurance of eventual human perfection.

Until recently, the association of the claims of the ideology with the manifest advances of natural science and technology lent powerful support to this belief. The attainment of Communism, however, is by far the most important development the ideology envisages. Therefore, once a prediction of the time for attaining Communism has been publicly incorporated into the body of the ideology, indefinitely postponing the time is tantamount to renouncing the predictive power of the ideology. The problem, then, goes beyond mere disappointment of the citizenry; Soviet citizens could actually lose faith in Communist ideology.

Thus far, the regime appears to be temporizing, tacitly dropping the emphasis on attaining Communism, but avoiding a public revision of the timetable. Earlier faulty predictions could be explained away, since either they were made by theoreticians (like Marx and Lenin) who had not yet attained power, or (as in the case of Stalin's errors) they were not so intimately related to the sacrifices and aspirations of the Soviet people. The 1961 predictions are painfully contemporary; in view of the enormous publicity given to the program before 1965, it is hard to see how the present generation can be induced to forget these predictions. Moreover, since the regime that made them had enjoyed power for forty-four years, the Soviet population is not likely to forgive it its manifest inability to predict. Nevertheless, Marxism-Leninism has shown itself to be a remarkably persistent and flexible doctrine. Its skilled ideologues may yet find a way to restore its credibility.

Marxism-Leninism—A Dogma?

There is, however, another side to the unavowed flexibility of Marxist-Leninist doctrine. Because the basic tenets are actually subject to revision, there is no dogma in the true sense of the word. The dominant element in the Communist Party determines what is orthodox; those who cling to another interpretation, even one undisputed in earlier years, become heretics, and no exegetical appeal to the "classics" can save them. Obviously, this aspect of the ideology strengthens the absolutist claims of the current leadership. By opening up a broad area of ideological uncertainty, it also promotes a high degree of dynamism in the system. The Soviet Communist knows that he cannot justify himself by ideological orthodoxy; consequently, he tries to assure his position by maximum practical service to the regime and by anticipation of its shifting theoretical requirements. For the hard core of the regime's supporters, therefore, faith in the ideology as a consistent belief system is not the only basis for loyalty.

SUGGESTED READING • CHAPTER 2

The "classics" of Soviet ideology, according to the official definition, embrace the works of Karl Marx, Friedrich Engels, V. I. Lenin, and—until recently—Joseph Stalin. Most are available in English, but many of them are of interest mainly to specialists in social thought. The few listed below are among the most important for an understanding of the U.S.S.R. and are most readily comprehensible to the nonspecialist.

LENIN, VLADIMIR I. *Imperialism* and *State and Revolution*. New York: The Vanguard Press, 1929, and many other editions. Two of the basic political works of the founder of Bolshevism. *Imperialism* tries to show that capitalism is to blame for colonialism and war, and that revolution will occur in the "weakest link," while *State and Revolution* sets forth Lenin's concept of the Party and the revolution it is to accomplish.

STALIN, JOSEPH V. *The History of the Communist Party of the Soviet*

Union (Bolsheviks). New York: International Publishers, 1939, and many later editions also published by Communist agencies. A completely distorted history, but important as the book of indoctrination under Stalin. The section on "Dialectical and Historical Materialism" is a summary of Stalin's version of Marxism.

STALIN, JOSEPH V. *Problems of Leninism.* New York: International Publishers, 1942. An earlier and more extensive ideological work. Since Stalin's death, a new *History of the Communist Party of the Soviet Union* (Moscow: Foreign Languages Publishing House, 1960) has superseded Stalin's version. While not yet a "classic," the new book (which is scarcely less distorted) plays an important part in current Soviet indoctrination.

Critical works by non-Communists:

HISTORICUS. "Stalin on Revolution," *Foreign Affairs,* January, 1949. A brief but revealing discussion of Stalin's real consistency in advocating world revolution.

HUNT, ROBERT N. C. *The Theory and Practice of Communism.* New York: The Macmillan Company, 1954; Baltimore: Pelican paperback, 1964. The best survey of the development of Communist ideas from Marx through Stalin.

MARCUSE, HERBERT. *Soviet Marxism.* New York: Columbia University Press, 1958. A personal but stimulating interpretation.

MEYER, ALFRED G. *Leninism.* Cambridge, Mass.: Harvard University Press, 1957; New York: Praeger paperback, 1962. A comprehensive and objective analysis of Lenin's theories, related to his personality and political objectives.

MONNEROT, JULES. *Sociology and Psychology of Communism.* Boston: Beacon Press, 1953. This study by a French scholar is the most elaborate presentation of the concept that Communism is a "secular religion."

MOORE, BARRINGTON. *Soviet Politics—the Dilemma of Power.* Cambridge, Mass.: Harvard University Press, 1950. A brilliant attempt to show how Bolshevik ideas changed when the Communists were confronted with the problems of running a great country.

WETTER, GUSTAV A. *Dialectical Materialism.* New York: Frederick A. Praeger, 1959. A thorough examination of the development of Soviet philosophical concepts (especially the philosophy of science) by a Jesuit priest who formerly directed the Vatican's Collegium Russicum.

3

THE PARTY

The Communist Party is the core institution of the Soviet political system. Much confusion results, however, from identification of this "party" with the familiar parties of pluralist political systems. In a pluralist system, there are almost always two or more parties. The leaders of each party assume the continued existence of at least one opposing party, though they devoutly hope to keep their opponents out of power, in the role of "loyal opposition." Each party acts as a legitimate institution for articulating the political demands of a number of groups in the society. In a multiparty system, the range of demands articulated by each such party is comparatively narrow, for every set of interests tends to be represented by a different party. In a two-party system, each party not only articulates a wide range of interests but also serves to "aggregate" these interests—that is, to combine and compromise them in a way that usually promotes the smooth functioning of the pluralist political system as a whole.

In its conception, the Soviet Communist Party was an entirely different phenomenon. As indicated in Chapter 2, Lenin regarded the Party as the indispensable instrument by which the Marxist vision of a perfect society was to be attained. From the outset, the Party was a conspiratorial instrument for overthrowing the existing Czarist political system rather than a legitimate instrument for articulating demands within the system; the compromises that inevitably attach to legitimacy were rejected by Lenin, who saw them as tantamount to "reformism." Following the Revolution, the Party was the essence of the "dictatorship of the proletariat," a role it held for four decades. In this capacity, the Party (which became officially known as the "Communist Party" in 1918, though the term "Bolshevik" was retained until 1952) was explicitly given the monopoly of political articulation; all other parties were suppressed. At the same time, Lenin and his followers rejected the concept of the single party as an overarching institution of interest aggregation, for they regarded the Party as a force to transform, rather than to mediate, the interests and the political culture of the existing society. The Communist Party became the institutional guardian and interpreter of the ideology and was charged with indoctrinating the population with the ideas and values that would make them psychologically capable of living under full Communism. All of these functions of the Party are avowed by the Soviet regime today. Indeed, the latest Party program appears to view the Party as immortal, for (unlike the state) it will not disappear, even after full Communism is attained.

In view of the enormous importance that Lenin ascribed to the Party, it is hard to imagine that it could ever have been eclipsed. Yet many observers have viewed Stalin's career as a victory over the Communist Party itself. There is much to recommend this view. Because of his bitter animosity toward the Old Bolsheviks, Lenin's companions, Stalin evidently distrusted the Party, which they symbolized. As an absolute dictator, he distrusted any institutional locus of power. Consequently, he limited the sway of the Party, devolving many functions in the execution of his will upon state organs, particularly (as will appear in Chapter 5) the police. It took, however, all of the power of an absolute ruler to reduce the scope of the Party. Even then, Stalin never tried to reduce the theoretical significance of the Party. Every Communist was taught that the Party was the only infallible guide to the course of history and that its command was beyond question. For the most part, the indoctrinating agencies of the Party (or agencies intimately associated with the Party indoctrination machine) transmitted the teachings of Marx, Engels, and Lenin, even though they were partially distorted by Stalin's reinterpretations. From his adolescence on, the Communist therefore is taught to accept the Party as the essential institution of the Soviet system.

As a result, it is scarcely surprising that the Party regained complete ascendancy soon after Stalin's death. This re-emergence of the Party as the dominant institutional force in the U.S.S.R. is very closely associated with the rise of Nikita Khrushchev. Even in Stalin's lifetime, Khrushchev had insisted on the paramount position of the Party: "The Party is responsible for everything. Whether it is Army work, Chekist [police] work, economic work, Soviet work—all is subordinate to the Party leadership, and if anyone thinks otherwise, that means he is no Bolshevik." Shortly after Stalin's death, Georgi Malenkov, who appeared to lead the field of possible successors, resigned as a member of the Party Secretariat while retaining the position of head of the Soviet Government. Khrushchev, on the other hand, became the highest Party officer. In retrospect, it is clear that the prestige and the power levers concentrated in the Party were major factors in enabling Khrushchev to win in the struggle for supreme authority in the U.S.S.R. Regardless of their rank in government agencies, other Soviet leaders were also Party members formally bound to obey orders issued in the name of the Party. Within each branch of the Soviet bureaucracy, many officials were tied to power alignments that led them to follow the Party leadership rather than their nominal superiors. Thus, in June, 1953, when the head of the police apparatus, Lavrenti Beria, sought to counter Party dominance, he was abandoned by many of the high-ranking police officers. A year and a half later (January, 1955), a Party meeting ordered Malenkov to resign as head of the government. He complied the following month. In 1957, the central economic directorates were fully subordinated to Party control. Later that year, the Party (vigorously supported by many high military officers) successfully demanded the removal of Marshal Georgi Zhukov, head of the Defense Ministry. Khrushchev's words were prophetic: "Army work, Chekist work, economic work, Soviet work—all is subordinate to the Party leadership."

Khrushchev himself was ousted from the leadership in October, 1964. Since then, the Party chief (Leonid Brezhnev) has not headed the Soviet Government, and central government officials appear to have regained a modest measure of power. As an institution, however, the Party remains pre-eminent. Khrushchev's ouster was carried out by a group in which Party officers heavily predominated and was formally ratified by a Party meeting. In the years following, the dominant role of the Party has been strongly reaffirmed and its directing bodies hailed as the loci of "collective leadership." In spite of its past record as an instrument for the attainment of personal dictatorship, there is no reason to think that the Party's institutional pre-eminence depends on the existence of personal rule.

MEMBERSHIP: STATUS ASPECTS

The preceding discussion suggests that the significance of the Party as an institution resides in its leadership. To a considerable extent, as will appear in Chapter 4, this is true. The role of the Party as a membership organization requires careful examination, however. In sheer size, the Soviet Communist Party resembles the mass membership parties of pluralist societies. The Soviet Party membership is now 13 million (including .6 million candidate or probationary members), constituting about 9 per cent of the adult population of the U.S.S.R. Nevertheless, Soviet writers have always explicitly rejected the term "mass organization" for the Party. Instead, they follow Lenin's prescription that selection of members be made with great care, so that the Party may act as a leaven within the whole social structure rather than become submerged in it. In sharp contrast to pluralist parties, the Communist Party does not solicit volunteer adherents, but chooses its members. The mere fact of the enrollment of nearly all eminent Soviet citizens provides a propaganda advantage. The regime constantly boasts that the outstanding citizens are Communists and uses this assertion as a proof that the Party embodies the best of Soviet society. Consequently, the prize-winning physicist, the record-breaking milkmaid, the popular novelist, the renowned Arctic explorer, are all prime targets for recruitment into the Party. In crisis situations such as war, extraordinary effort (to the point of complete neglect of the ideological background or intellectual capacity of the candidates) is devoted to bringing all "heroic" figures into the Party to serve as examples to their fellows. Ordinarily, however, prospective members are carefully screened. Each must be recommended by three persons who have already been Party members for at least five years. In accordance with the principle that a prime duty of each Communist is to "safeguard the Party against the infiltration of persons unworthy of the lofty title of Communist," sponsors are held responsible for a new member's derelictions.

Despite the care exercised in selection, the sense in which rank-and-file Communists constitute the "elite" of Soviet society is limited. Membership is, of course, a requisite for selection as a Party official, and it is useful, if not always essential, for advancement in the state bureaucracy. At times, Party membership helps in a professional or intellectual career, but the need to utilize all highly qualified persons in such work limits the degree to which political preference is feasible. Rank-and-file membership by no means connotes membership in the ruling circles of the Soviet Union; as will be shown below, such circles are confined to a much more select group. In effect, therefore, ordinary Party membership is more an honor than a privilege, and one which carries with it the onerous burdens of constant study, indoctrinating assignments, and occasional transfer to unattractive posts. Once in the Party, members must carry these burdens diligently if not cheerfully, or face expulsion. It is far worse to be an ex-Party member than a person who has never joined the Party, for the former are pariahs in Soviet society. In recent years, to be sure, expulsions have been few. The annual rate of expulsions is about 60,000, or .05 per cent of the total membership. But the person who views Party duties as distasteful is shrewder if he never becomes a member, and in fact many talented Soviet citizens do evade joining.

Slightly over one-sixth of the Party members have some higher education. They, plus those with specialized secondary education, constitute about one-third of the Party membership —a disproportionate component if one considers that such "experts" constitute only one-tenth of the entire adult population. However, approximately one-fourth of the Party members have only elementary educations. This is an additional indication that membership in the Party, while selective, is not confined to those holding high-status jobs. In recent years, there has been renewed emphasis upon enlisting ordinary factory workers, though white-collar workers continue to predominate. Proportionately, the rural areas have less than half as many Party members as the cities, and there are probably only a fourth as many among the "dirt farmers" or peasants. On the other hand, physicians and teachers are three times as heavily represented in the Party as in the general population, while such favored—and strategic—groups as engineers and military officers are six or seven times as strongly represented as ordinary occupations. Officials (both of the state and the

Party bureaucracies) are of course even more heavily represented. Women constitute only one-fifth of the members, although, because of heavy war losses among males, they constitute well over half of the adult Soviet population. As indicated in Chapter 6 and its accompanying table, some nationality groups, such as Russians and Transcaucasians, are much more heavily represented than nationalities such as the Central Asians.

Membership: Functions

The symbolic function of Party membership has already been noted: Enrollment of the "best" citizens demonstrates that the Party comprises the best of Soviet society. The general Party membership is also highly important to the regime as a reservoir of disposable manpower. As noted earlier, every Communist must accept assignments made by the leadership. In a crisis, therefore, the leadership can freely command millions of the most energetic and talented Soviet citizens. For example, every few years, tens of thousands of urban Communists have been sent out to the villages to stimulate lagging agricultural production and to perfect political organization.

The principal activity of the Party member as a stimulator of production is carried out, however, within his primary Party organization. The Party has always maintained that these basic units should be formed in places of work; today, this principle is generally applied. Of about 340,000 primary organizations, 80,000 are in factories, transportation, and the like, while 50,000 are on farms. The remainder are in various institutions, administrative offices, and military formations. The last are especially important, for, together with the deputy commander for political affairs (a military officer dependent upon the Party), the Party organization provides the regime with a pervasive curb upon the military. Whatever the agency of the Soviet system, the primary organization is charged with general supervision of activities. Ordinarily, the primary organization may not command an agricultural agency to take specific action, but its advice is often compelling. In a military unit, on the other hand, the Party organization may not even discuss a purely military decision. Most primary-organization policy actions have an effect somewhat in-between these extremes, and are consequently difficult to define. The design, however, is to expose officials to a constant flow of pressure and criticism from Party members who are most familiar with the officials' operations. At the same time, the primary organization is designed to stimulate its own membership (which almost always includes the officials concerned) to more strenuous efforts to further the regime's objectives.

The primary Party organization's significance is enhanced by its power to make the initial decision on the admission and expulsion of members. Admission or expulsion must be confirmed by the next-higher Party echelon, however, and an expelled member may appeal to the Party Control Commission attached to the Central Committee of the Communist Party of the Soviet Union. Between 1956 and 1961, 70,000 appeals were made; 15,000 of these resulted in the reversal of the expulsion decisions.

A third most important function of the general membership is indoctrination. The Party is the basic institution for manipulating the political culture both of its own members and of Soviet society in general. Every member has the duty to "master Marxist-Leninist theory, raise his ideological level, and contribute to the molding and rearing of the man of Communist society." The most systematic and concentrated indoctrination program is directed at the Communists themselves. Elementary political education (frequently provided in short-term evening courses) is designed to provide a minimal knowledge of Marxism-Leninism, Party history, and current

policy questions. Intermediate training includes more abstruse
ideological materials and emphasizes independent study. The
"evening universities of Marxism-Leninism" have been an important part of this stage of training. Advanced training is
designed especially for the "executive cadres" of Party and
state bureaucracies. For these officials, there is a whole series
of full-time schools, culminating in the Higher Party School
in Moscow, which has a regular four-year curriculum at the
university level. These schools heighten indoctrination at the
same time that they provide practical training in public administration and political technique. Their instruction is
regarded as so important that middle-aged men holding re-
sponsibilities as great as those of the governor of an American
state are sent to the schools for retraining before being given
new assignments.

All levels of Party indoctrination are designed not only to
indoctrinate the Party member but to prepare him to indoctrinate others with the current policy "line" and with the
concepts and values the regime believes to be essential attri-
butes of members of the future Communist society. At an
early date, the Soviet leadership intuitively grasped the sociological principle that transmission of ideas is most effectively
accomplished by "opinion leaders" who are in face-to-face contact with small groups. Communist Party members constitute
the backbone of the huge force of "agitators" who implement
this principle. During a rest period in a factory workshop, for
example, a Communist agitator will read an editorial from
the Party newspaper, *Pravda*, embodying the current "line,"
to his fellow workers, lest they idle away their time. While
there is evidence that such emphasis on indoctrination often
irritates the average Soviet citizen, the constant reiteration of
the regime's viewpoint, unchallenged by any opposing opinion,
is bound to induce a considerable measure of acceptance. Undoubtedly, the "oral" agitation program vastly increases the
impact of printed indoctrinating material.

THE PARTY'S AUXILIARY ORGANIZATIONS

Though the Party is the principal indoctrination force, it is not alone in undertaking the enormous task of preparing Soviet society for complete Communism. Large as the Party now is, the regime still excludes the vast majority of Soviet citizens from Party membership. On the other hand, the regime does not wish to deal with all those who are outside the Party as a single, undifferentiated mass. Consequently, several mass organizations have been established outside the Party framework, but actually operating under its close and direct supervision.

The most important mass organization is the Communist Youth League, or Komsomol. The Party itself is definitely an adult organization. A slight majority of the members are under forty, but nearly one-fourth are past fifty and there is a small but growing group of elderly, retired members. It is true that one may secure admission to the Party at the early age of eighteen, but all who are admitted under the age of twenty-three must have been members of Komsomol. The latter organization serves, therefore, as a screening agency in which most prospective Party members are indoctrinated and observed before the crucial step of admission to the Party. Between 1953 and 1963, 30 million youths entered the Komsomol, but only 2.5 million of them became Party members. From the regime's standpoint, however, Komsomol membership was by no means wasted on the 90 per cent who did not enter the Party. The present membership of 23 million probably comprises a majority of the adolescents (aged 14–18) and a substantial minority of the 19–26 age group. In any society, these age groups are especially sensitive and susceptible to the influence of ideas. The Komsomol institution is designed to see that they are exposed to heavy, though somewhat elementary, indoctrination. Komsomol members are expected to have an acquaintance with all ideological documents, from Marx's *Communist Manifesto* to resolutions of the latest Party congress. To a considerable extent, however, more vivid works, such as Lenin's biography and the memoirs of war heroes, provide implicit models for the younger readers.

The organizational structure of the Komsomol is modeled on that of the Party. Top officers are Party members, for a young person who enters the Party can retain Komsomol membership until twenty-eight if he is elected to office. At lower levels, few Party members do remain active in the Komsomol; only 2 per cent of its primary party organizations are headed by Party members. In spite of the regime's efforts, there appears to be an increasing tendency to regard the Komsomol as a boring and restrictive institution. In many secondary and higher educational institutions, and in the armed forces, Komsomol membership in primary organizations is almost obligatory. Precisely because it includes such a large proportion of the relevant age groups, Komsomol membership does not have the honorific significance of Party membership. Yet, membership entails almost as many burdens as Party membership. Komsomol youths constituted a high proportion of those sent to farm the "virgin lands" in the 1950's. Members are frequently called for short-term work details as well as for agitation tasks. The Komsomol tries to become popular by organizing recreational activities like open-air dances, but even these are often injected with an element of propaganda. Still more objectionable to many youths is the role of the Komsomol as a guardian of morals, manners, and, of course, political fidelity. In recent years, Komsomol patrols have been assigned auxiliary police power to control youths in the streets and in places of amusement—in some cases, going so far as to ban "loud" sport shirts.

The Komsomol also exercises tutelage over the Pioneers, the organization for children of primary school age. According to Soviet sources, all children in the 10–15 age group belong to the Pioneers. While many of their activities (games, camping, and the like) resemble those of Western youth groups like the Boy Scouts and the Campfire Girls, the Pioneer groups are also an important element in the indoctrination process. Recent Soviet reports suggest, however, that even these children are bored by the overorganized activity that is as much a characteristic of the Pioneers as of other Soviet institutions.

Numerically, the Soviet trade unions, with some 65 million members, are even more obviously mass organizations than the Komsomol. The massive size of the trade unions has been useful to the Soviet regime in its foreign policy—their large representation in the World Federation of Trade Unions enabled Communists to gain control over this international organization soon after World War II. Soviet trade unions also have important domestic functions. The usual units of trade-union organization are factories, with factory unions grouped both by industry and by region. Practically the entire white-collar and industrial labor force is enrolled in unions, which have been delegated minor functions in supervising work conditions, such as safety inspection, and job benefits, such as vacations and sports facilities. The trade unions have little practical effect on economic policy, but they do play a part, though a very restricted one, in setting wage scales and reviewing dismissals of employees. The trade unions' role in stimulating production and in promoting "socialist emulation" is greater than its role in determining economic policy. Through their factory clubs and frequent meetings, the unions also directly engage in the indoctrination process, though apparently a much more restricted one than that assigned to the Komsomol. Even Soviet sources class only two-fifths of the trade union members as "activists," though the regime regards "public work in the trade unions [as] a good school for working people, fostering their Communist education and strengthening their concern for the interests of state and society."

A more important indoctrination agency (not officially

classed as a mass organization) is the Society for Knowledge. With a membership of 1 million, the Society formally resembles an adult-education organization. The bulk of its work is carried on by a body of 75,000 lecturers, most of whom serve on a part-time basis. The lectures, which are often delivered at factories and on farms, cover a wide spectrum of subjects: the Communist Party program, peace, space exploration, and technological advances. Many lectures are undoubtedly designed to impart practical knowledge as well as to indoctrinate. Probably the most important theme, however, is "debunking" religion.

Finally, one should mention DOSAAF—the conventional abbreviation of the organization now entitled the Volunteer Society for Cooperation with the Army, Air Force, and Navy. DOSAAF has performed a variety of tasks, including civil defense functions, entertainment of servicemen, and cooperation in the indoctrination of military personnel. Its role in fostering military-type sports for school children is especially important.

ORGANIZATIONAL PRINCIPLES

In theory, the organization of the Communist Party is based on Lenin's principle of "democratic centralism." At the Twenty-third Party Congress, Brezhnev defined democratic centralism as "free opinion in deciding questions and iron discipline after a decision is taken." A few years earlier, another Party spokesman explained the principle more elaborately:

> In the course of the discussion, a predominant point of view emerges from among many to serve as a basis for the decision adopted. The minority has the right to defend its opinion until a decision is adopted, but when it is adopted the minority must submit to the majority. The principle of democratic centralism

offers the opportunity for the broadest participation of the Party masses in working out Party policy. But, at the same time, it closes all the loopholes through which all kinds of individualistic and anarchistic views and habits might sneak into the Party, it protects the Party from cliques and splits. . . .

There can be genuine authority of leadership only in a centralized party. And this is highly important. There are still people among us who try to sneak bourgeois laxity and loquacity into our midst, who try to undermine the foundations of the socialist society. The Party has crushed these tendencies in the past and is resolutely crushing them now.*

Each echelon of the Party is supposed to be free to discuss a matter until a final decision has been reached by a higher echelon. The present statutes allow "broad" Party discussion only if the need is recognized by several high-level Party organizations or by the Central Committee itself. In practice, as will be discussed in greater detail, this means the central authorities are free to permit or forbid discussion on any matters that impinge on general policy. On the other hand, lower Party organizations are permitted, and indeed bound, to discuss implementation of policy at their own level and below. "Criticism" and "self-criticism" are characteristic features of this discussion, through which inefficient or delinquent members are brought to confess their sins and, presumably, mend their ways.

In a very similar fashion, the nominally free elections in the Party organizations are guided from above. Ostensibly, the primary organization, for example, annually elects a directing bureau and a secretary (usually not a full-time official), who serve as its chief officers. Every two years, the primary organization also elects delegates to a conference at the next-higher level, the rayon or district. Our information about the actual

---

* V. Klochko, "The Leninist Principle of Democratic Centralism," *Partiinaya Zhizn*, No. 14 (July, 1963), 22–28, as translated in *Current Digest of the Soviet Press*, XV, No. 38, 25–26.

conduct of these elections is far from complete. It is clear, however, that the *nomenklatura* system applies to elected as well as to appointed officials in the Party organization. Under this system, higher officials make personnel assignments for a designated group of lower Party organizations. In making these assignments, the personnel officials not only take into account individual qualifications of Party members, but "balance" such factors as age levels of a class of lower officials to give each age group the impression that it is adequately represented. Obviously, the *nomenklatura* system would not work if the choice of important categories of officials were left to an entirely free elective process. Apparently, the procedure actually used is to "suggest" to the Party body that it elect a specific slate—sometimes including persons who are unknown to the Party members participating in the elections. Before many important local elections, Party officials from Moscow arrive as visitors; they deliver speeches to the Party meetings, and, either openly or covertly, pass on the wishes of the central authorities concerning the slate to be elected. Obviously, these "suggestions" deprive democratic centralism of significance in many circumstances, though blatant manipulation of elections is occasionally criticized by the Party press, and lower Party meetings apparently do reject obnoxious candidates from time to time.

The level of Party organization just above the primary organization is a geographical subdivision, the rayon or district (medium-sized cities correspond to districts). There are 3,000 districts. In each district, a conference of delegates from the dozens of primary Party organizations takes place every two years. The conference formally elects a committee, which, in turn, elects a bureau and three secretaries. The latter are full-time officials of the Party apparatus. The district conference also elects delegates to the next-higher level, the oblast or province (in some cases a large city or a special nationality unit). There are nearly 200 such territorial units throughout the U.S.S.R. The provincial conference elects a committee, which, in turn, elects its bureau and secretaries (three to five in number) every two years. Every four years, the provincial conference continues the pyramidal process of indirect election by choosing delegates to a Union Republic Party congress.* The republic congresses elect central committees, which, in turn, elect bureaus and secretaries. In addition, every four years (the time intervals have been approximately but not rigidly observed in recent years), conferences in the provinces and in the smaller republics, elect delegates to the "All-Union" Congress of the Communist Party of the Soviet Union itself. The Congress elects the Central Committee and the Central Inspection Commission. The Central Committee then elects the General Secretary, several other secretaries, the Politburo, and the Party Control Commission.

One may well ask at this point whether the purpose of this elaborate system of elections is merely to preserve the appearance of democratic centralism, a purpose that may well be achieved as far as the feelings of the ordinary Party member are concerned. As noted in Chapter 2, the concept of democratic centralism had little meaning even in Lenin's time, for the conspiratorial nature of the pre-Revolutionary Bolshevik Party prevented regular elections. Never having known anything resembling the hotly contested free elections that characterize Western political parties, it is likely that many Soviet Communists do not realize how hollow their "inner-Party democracy" is.

There are other purposes, however. The considerable investment of man-hours of important officials (for the congress and conference delegations embrace nearly all major Party

---

* The largest republic, the Russian Soviet Federated Socialist Republic (R.S.F.S.R.) has no congress; on the other hand, the ten smallest republics have no provinces between the district and the republic levels.

VERTICAL ORGANIZATION AND SUPERVISORY FUNCTIONS IN THE CPSU

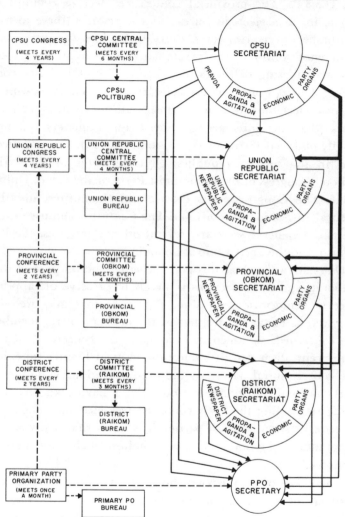

and state officials in the U.S.S.R.) is justified by the experience these officials get in discussing problems with their peers and superiors, for higher officials obtain some idea of "grass-roots" feeling by talking with provincial officials. Doubtless for this reason and to preserve an impression of "inner-Party democracy," higher authorities have recently criticized meetings in which all speeches are prearranged. Through personal contact —especially if it retains a measure of spontaneity—top officials have a chance to evaluate the loyalty and ability of promising subordinates. But spontaneity cannot go too far, especially at the top of the Party pyramid. The major assemblies, especially the All-Union Congress, provide a superb forum for setting forth and publicizing the Party line of the moment. Nearly 5,000 Congress delegates, meeting for only ten or twelve days, could not (even in the absence of manipulation) debate and reach decisions on complex issues. But they provide an impressive backdrop for the speeches of the major leaders of the Soviet regime and an appearance of "monolithic" support for the regime's policies. The occasion is, in fact, so useful that All-Union congresses in recent years have several times been the scene of proclamations of major policy.

SUGGESTED READING • CHAPTER 3

Most general histories of Russia (such as those listed in Chapter 1) discuss the Communist Party; so do the specialized works listed in the following chapters. The books listed below are mainly general works on the Soviet system that stress the role of the Party.

FAINSOD, MERLE. *How Russia Is Ruled.* Rev. ed. Cambridge, Mass.: Harvard University Press, 1963. Probably the best book on the operation of the Soviet political system.

HAZARD, JOHN N. *The Soviet System of Government.* Chicago: University of Chicago Press, 1964. Concise, authoritative, and highly readable, this is an outstanding general survey.

INKELES, ALEX, BAUER, RAYMOND A., and KLUCKHOHN, CLYDE. *How the Soviet System Works.* Cambridge, Mass.: Harvard University

Press, 1957; New York: Vintage paperback, 1960. Directed more to social and cultural elements than to political elements, this book supplements the other works listed in this section.

McCLOSKY, HERBERT, and TURNER, JOHN E. *The Soviet Dictatorship.* New York: McGraw-Hill Book Company, 1966. A massive treatment of Soviet political institutions.

MEYER, ALFRED G. *The Soviet Political System: An Interpretation.* New York: Random House, 1965. An analytic approach comparing Soviet politics to those of a large corporation.

SCOTT, DEREK J. R. *Russian Political Institutions.* New York: Rinehart and Company, 1957; Praeger paperback, 1961. An excellent British survey of Soviet institutions.

TOWSTER, JULIAN. *Political Power in the U.S.S.R.* London and New York: Oxford University Press, 1948. In spite of its early date, this book remains valuable for its illuminating discussion of the theoretical bases of Soviet institutions.

The following books are somewhat more specialized in character:

ARMSTRONG, JOHN A. *The Politics of Totalitarianism.* New York: Random House, 1961. A detailed examination of the Party and Soviet politics between 1934 and 1960.

FISHER, RALPH. *Pattern for Soviet Youth.* New York: Columbia University Press, 1959. A detailed history of the Communist Youth League (Komsomol).

KASSOF, ALLEN. *The Soviet Youth Program: Regimentation and Rebellion.* Cambridge, Mass.: Harvard University Press, 1965. A sociological study of the Communist Youth League and related activities.

INKELES, ALEX. *Public Opinion in Soviet Russia.* Cambridge, Mass.: Harvard University Press, 1950. The only comprehensive treatment in English of the Party mechanisms for indoctrination.

RESHETAR, JOHN S. *A Concise History of the Communist Party of the Soviet Union.* New York: Frederick A. Praeger, 1960. A much briefer survey than Schapiro's, but very useful and available in paperback.

SCHAPIRO, LEONARD. *The Communist Party of the Soviet Union.* New York: Random House, 1960; Vintage paperback, 1963. A thorough and penetrating history of the Party from its beginnings to the Khrushchev era.

CENTRAL ORGANIZATION OF THE SOVIET COMMUNIST PARTY

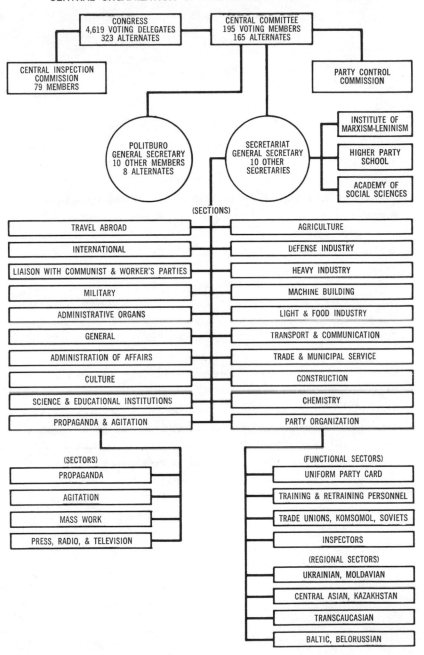

4

THE APPARATUS

In Communist theory, the Soviet political system is a mono-lith. The Party is the infallible interpreter of the historical process and, consequently, the irrefutable guide to action. The doctrine does not recognize the existence of conflicting interests that the political system must adjust and compromise. Operating under the principle of democratic centralism, the Party leadership acts as the supreme decision-making body, with other Soviet institutions faithfully executing Party policies.

In fact, as we have already seen, the Soviet political system has been frequently racked by severe conflicts. These conflicts have involved prominent leaders and those lower officials who, for one reason or another, have been their adherents, but, in all cases, the divergent groups were centered around segments of the Soviet structure of formal, large-scale institutions. In other words, the conflicts were forms of bureaucratic politics. What Communist ideology, as an element of political culture, accomplished was to keep the resolution of these conflicts largely within the institutional framework of the Communist Party. Other institutions may serve as power bases or develop divergent interests, but rivalries among them are formally resolved by Party bodies. Despite the monolithic nature Lenin ascribed to it, one may view the Party as the legitimate institution for aggregating interests and demands in the Soviet system. These interests are distinguished from those of a pluralist society in that they derive from segments of a formally unified bureaucracy rather than from formally independent groups. Consequently, the interests acquire legitimacy only insofar as they are expressed in terms (usually implicit) which stress the values of the system as a whole and deny distinctive interest positions. Furthermore, because of Lenin's extreme aversion to factionalism (or, as he put it, "fractionalism"), no bureaucratic group may openly constitute an alignment even if its avowed purpose is to promote the general welfare of the system rather than some particular interest. In spite of the manifest existence of divergent positions and bitter conflict throughout the history of the Soviet system, the official doctrine still condemns factionalists in the sharpest terms. The core of the charge against the "anti-Party" group of 1957 was that its members had met secretly (in the office of the head of the Soviet Government) to concert a program and a plan for implementing it. At lower levels, officials have taken action against Party members for merely failing to report casual discussions of concerted protests to the authorities. A crucial question, therefore, is: How can decision-making involving divergent viewpoints take place in the Soviet system?

As was described in Chapter 3, the Congress is the formal supreme body; but its brief sessions and infrequent meetings would, aside from all other factors, disqualify it from making basic decisions. Consequently, one must look elsewhere for the real locus of Soviet power. During nearly all of the period between the Revolution and 1964, most observers found no difficulty in identifying the decision-maker with the personal dictator: Lenin, Stalin, Khrushchev. In retrospect, at least, it seems clear that decision-making was a much more complex affair during Lenin's and Khrushchev's ascendancy and that, even under Stalin, decision-making was less centralized than was imagined. Nevertheless, the concentration of power in the hands of these men was enormous. Some observers have superficially concluded that this concentration is sanctioned or even demanded by Communist ideology, which, until 1961, called for a "dictatorship of the proletariat." In fact, this formula never implied that an *individual* was to be dictator. Even under Stalin, "collective leadership" was occasionally extolled, and the phrase has become the constant refrain of his successors.

While some observers have contended that Lenin envisaged the necessity for one-man rule, probably most students of his writings agree that this was not the case. *In practice,* however, Lenin did make most of the basic decisions of the Soviet regime during his time. Stalin ruled (at least after 1937) as an absolute despot. As far as he was able, he made all important (and many trivial) decisions himself. He clothed his rule in secrecy, often avoiding the discussion of pending matters even with his own hand-picked circle of high officials. He instigated a campaign of adulation for his person that has rarely been exceeded in a modern country. Stalin was slavishly acclaimed as the greatest genius of mankind, omniscient and infallible. At the same time, he sedulously undermined any force, institutional or personal, that could possibly compete with him for power. He humiliated his associates in numerous ways, and in hundreds of cases had them executed without even publishing accusations against them. This was personal dictatorship in the most absolute sense of the term. Yet even Stalin was unable to direct all aspects of the vastly complex technological society the U.S.S.R. had become by 1953. Consequently, he had to rely on lieutenants to make countless minor decisions as well as to execute his own commands.

As indicated in the preceding chapter, none of Stalin's lieutenants was immediately able to assume full control of the Soviet system. Between March, 1953, and January, 1955 (and, to a lesser extent, until June, 1957), a real "collective leadership," based on the Politburo,* made many basic decisions. This was, in some respects, a return to the pre-1937 situation. In Lenin's later years, and during the first decade of Stalin's predomi-

---

* Officially designated the Party Presidium between 1952 and 1966.

nance, the Politburo met very frequently and considered a wide range of questions. In Stalin's later years, however, it almost ceased to function. For a time after his death, it seemed that the Politburo was to be the select committee ruling the Soviet Union.

As time went on, however, the post-Stalin Politburo members found it harder and harder to exert influence. In every modern political system there is probably a tendency to have one man, whether he be an American President or a British Prime Minister, symbolize authority. In the Soviet system, this tendency is vastly enhanced by the absence of legitimate institutional mechanisms for articulating and resolving differences. In addition, Stalin's approach to losers in policy disputes—death or utter disgrace—continued, even after his death, to exert a powerful influence reinforcing the lack of restraint in power struggles. Under these circumstances, it was probably decisive that, as early as the spring of 1953, Khrushchev acquired the dominant position in the Party apparatus—the body of full-time officials that not only carries on the day-to-day *execution* of decisions but, as described in Chapter 3, manipulates elections and discussions in Party meetings. Because the apparatus performs these key functions, any group that opposes the apparatus is likely to be outmaneuvered; its adherents will not be elected to formal decision-making assemblies like the Congress, and efforts to concert policies opposed to those of the apparatus will be denounced as factionalism. Under the Party rules, the Politburo has, it is true, a legitimate place in the decision-making process. As long, therefore, as Khrushchev's rivals constituted its majority, they occupied a strong position. But the Politburo is not formally the supreme decision-making body.

In the long intervals between congresses (which, in any case, are too cumbersome and too brief in duration to play an important part in decisions), supreme authority is formally del-

egated to the Central Committee. After Stalin died, the
Central Committee was regularly hailed as the repository of
collective leadership. Most of the important officials of the
U.S.S.R. were then, and still are, among its several hundred
members and alternates. They are drawn from all major segments of the bureaucracy—state, economic, military, police—
but the Party apparatus predominates. It was at a plenum of
the Central Committee that Malenkov was secretly ordered
to resign as head of government, and it was the plenums that
constituted the forums for Khrushchev's principal policy de-
partures.

In the years between 1953 and 1957, there was a considerable turnover in membership of the Central Committee.
Undoubtedly Khrushchev, as chief of the apparatus, was able
to take advantage of this turnover to install his followers. On
the whole, however, it appears that his success with the Central
Committee derived less from manipulation of its membership than from its members' conviction that he was the aspir-
ant for top leadership most in accord with their interests.
Khrushchev's rivals (especially Malenkov) had been more
closely associated with the most repugnant features of Stalin's
rule, especially his destruction of 70 per cent of the Central
Committee elected in 1934. Like most apparatus members,
Khrushchev had been more intimately involved with bread-
and-butter Party affairs at the regional level than with covert
manipulation in Moscow. The Central Committee members
may have believed that Khrushchev, who was several years
older than Malenkov, would not have enough time to repeat
Stalin's crafty, step-by-step elimination of the Party leaders.
Moreover, he was relatively popular with foreign Communists,
especially Yugoslavia's Tito, and had established the image of
a dynamic figure.

In the spring of 1957, Khrushchev took two decisive steps
against his rivals. He secured Central Committee approval of

a sweeping scheme for reorganizing the bureaucracy that supervised industry. Instead of primary reliance on centralized ministries in Moscow, a "sovnarkhoz" ("council of people's economy") in each province was assigned primary responsibility. The cumbersome ministries were long overdue for reorganization, but, from an efficiency standpoint, the more than one hundred sovnarkhozes were too numerous. What the "reform" accomplished was to break up the central government apparatus associated with Moscow and to put industrial control under the supervision of Khrushchev's allies in the provincial Party apparatus. Having undermined their bureaucratic support, Khrushchev moved directly against his rivals by threatening to expose their complicity in Stalin's brutal annihilation of earlier Party leaders. In desperation, Khrushchev's opponents used their Politburo majority to demand his resignation. Citing the fact that he had been elected by the Central Committee, Khrushchev refused. A special Central Committee plenum, hastily assembled with the aid of the military command in June, 1957, overwhelmingly endorsed Khrushchev. His opponents were expelled from all major posts, though in some cases the expulsions were deliberately postponed to conceal the full extent of the Politburo's opposition. A new Politburo, composed mainly of Khrushchev's close associates, was elected. It appeared that Khrushchev had repeated the first stage of Stalin's move toward absolute dictatorship. But, seven years later, he was just as overwhelmingly rejected by a Central Committee whose membership, in 1964, was very much the same as it had been in 1957.

We do not know all of the grounds for this sweeping reversal, but the major reasons seem clear. Probably Khrushchev never had as much power as outside observers thought. Yet, he was identified with a number of dramatic policy decisions, including major changes in agriculture and an aggressive assertion of Communist interests abroad. As long as these policies appeared promising, Khrushchev was almost indispensable as a symbol of Soviet authority. When poor harvests and foreign-policy reverses (like the Cuban missile crisis) occurred, his value as a prestige symbol diminished and he became more of a liability than an asset. At the same time, it appears he infringed on the interests of a decisive portion of the Party apparatus. As early as 1956, Khrushchev sponsored a division of the apparatus between the Russian and the non-Russian republics. In 1962, he introduced a further division between the agricultural and the industrial sectors of control. This complicated rearrangement was confusing and burdensome for established Party officials, and of dubious value from an efficiency standpoint. Khrushchev's bifurcation of the apparatus may have appeared to many officials as a scheme to "divide and conquer." Even if its real purpose was to bring younger men with better technical educations into the apparatus, bifurcation did, in fact, drastically reduce the scope of the authority of most established Party officials.

It is hardly surprising that the established officials, who constituted the dominant group in the Central Committee, reacted sharply. In October, 1964, by a process that is still unclear, the Politburo turned against Khrushchev. Another hastily summoned Central Committee plenum deprived him of his major posts. In the succeeding months, bifurcation was completely reversed. Indeed, in many respects, the organization of the Party was turned back to forms that had prevailed before Khrushchev became its chief and, in some ways, to even earlier models. Most of the new, younger apparatus appointees were reduced to subordinate rank; the 1966 Congress confirmed the established officials in their dominant Central Committee role.

Since 1964, real collective leadership appears to have prevailed. The principal Party and government posts are separated, and the Politburo apparently discusses the most important questions. Yet, it is still too soon to tell whether this arrangement can be maintained long enough to acquire legitimacy. The Party leader can still appeal to the Central Committee against a Politburo majority. But the Central Committee can only function in times of crisis. Normally, its numerous members are scattered across the whole of the Soviet Union (indeed, a considerable number are ambassadors abroad). Its regular plenums take place only two or three times a year and usually last only a few days. Published records of the plenums indicate that they are characterized by set speeches rather than by free discussion. While all of the bureaucratic interest groups are represented in the Central Committee, as yet their representation is only virtual: Central Committee members are drawn from all segments of the Soviet bureaucracy, but they do not serve as the delegates of these segments.

Under these circumstances, the Central Committee can hardly be either the locus of ordinary decision-making or the recognized aggregating institution of the Soviet system. What the Central Committee can do—though two precedents do not adequately establish its authority—is to act as a legitimizing institution for leadership change. If this authority can be firmly established, the severity of risks to the system that arise from unrestrained factional disputes and protracted succession crises will be greatly diminished. In other words, the establishment of legitimacy will enhance the stability of the political system. In that case, it is almost inevitable that the Central Committee will, through more frequent, lengthier, and more flexible meetings, assume a larger role in on-going decision-making.

THE SECRETARIAT

Speculation on the future role of the Central Committee should not obscure the present reality. The Politburo still makes the day-to-day (and even month-to-month) decisions.

These decisions are implemented by the Secretariat, which apparently initiates most of them. Indeed, while the top level of the Secretariat is no longer dominant in the Politburo, it is still strongly represented there.

With the exception of the General Secretary (Brezhnev), each of the secretaries exercises supervision over a specific sphere of operations, but no secretary is permanently assigned to a definite activity; shifts and recombinations of spheres are frequent. Below this level, however, the divisions of the Secretariat, though occasionally redesignated, are relatively stable. Two sections appear to perform routine internal tasks for the Secretariat. The remaining sections are organized according to specific areas of activity and are designed to perform broad, general functions for the Soviet system and to supervise limited areas of Soviet society and foreign affairs.

The Administrative Organs Section supervises the general state bureaucracy. There are nine sections for economic activities. The International Section supervises relations with Communist parties in countries not dominated by Communist regimes; the Section for Liaison with Communist and Worker's Parties of Socialist Countries, as its title indicates, deals with the Communist-bloc countries. The Military Section (identical with the Main Political Administration of the Defense Ministry) supervises political officers in the armed forces. The director of the Military Section is not only a Party official but a general officer in the armed forces. Through him, the network of political officers in the armed forces is subordinated to the Secretariat as well as to the line military officers—a powerful device for securing military subordination to the regime.

As is the case with the primary Party organizations and intermediate Party levels, Secretariat sections are not supposed to direct economic activity or the state bureaucracy. They are to oversee, stimulate, and check the other bureaucracies;

these, in turn, supposedly are free to administer their own areas of competence. Obviously, the line between interfering in administrative decisions and merely prodding administrators to take action is a thin one. Much depends on the balance of forces between state and Party officials. If the state economic directors have powerful friends among top members of the regime, Party influence is limited; if a segment of the economy is lagging and its formal directors are under severe criticism, the corresponding Party officials may assume practical direction. In the last three years, state economic directors appear to have regained a considerable measure of independence. Under these circumstances, direct intervention in industry by the Secretariat economic sections and lower Party levels is largely confined to peripheral matters such as indoctrination programs for workers, expediting of shipments, and smoothing over frictions between economic agencies. Some reports suggest that, in the industrial field, Party officials find even these duties burdensome. In agriculture, on the other hand, Party intervention has always been more direct and important. But with both agriculture and industry, each Secretariat section (assisted by lower levels of the Party apparatus) continues to perform for its corresponding economic sphere the *nomenklatura* function—the assignment of Party members to positions. Since the overwhelming majority of administrative personnel belongs to the Party, this function is crucial.

THE INDOCTRINATION MACHINERY

Important as the sections just described are, those dealing with indoctrination and ideology are clearly closer to the heart of Party operations. The Propaganda and Agitation Section is the heart of the indoctrination machine. Its propaganda subsection ("sector") is officially charged with the presentation of a complex theme to a limited group. It is especially concerned with the supervision of the training courses described earlier. The sector for agitation (officially described as the presentation of a few ideas to the mass of the population) supervises the enormous body of Party agitators. The sector on mass work is apparently concerned with indoctrination activities in the Komsomol, trade unions, and special-purpose organizations.

The work of the Propaganda and Agitation Section is also directly connected, through the sectors on central journals, publishing, and criticism, with indoctrination through the printed word and mass media. Most newspapers are directly operated by the Party. The major exception is the central newspaper, *Izvestia,* nominally the organ of the state; at times, it has exhibited some divergence from Party policy, but today it (and the numerous papers designed for special audiences) are fully subordinate to Party direction. Newspapers are important not only as vehicles for indoctrination, but as a major means for enforcing central Party standards on lower organizations. Reporters from high-level papers have the right of access to all lower-level offices and economic agencies; they may inspect the premises, examine records, and question employees. Consequently, they constitute a permanent body of roving inspectors who may drop in entirely unexpectedly upon a complacent lower official. Often these visits are prompted by letters to the editor from politically zealous or personally dissatisfied employees or clients of the agency concerned. If the reporter finds an unsatisfactory situation, he may not order corrective measures. But, after the approval of his editor (often in consultation with the Secretariat), the reporter may write a scathing article. Few officials can withstand an attack of this nature in, let us say, *Pravda.*

Pravda and the other central newspapers are by no means alone in performing this inspectional function. Each level of

Party organization down through the district has its own news-paper. Moreover, since a newspaper is not confined to criticizing agencies on or immediately below its own level, but may range down the organizational scale, agencies at the lower levels may be subject to unexpected visits and attacks by representatives of several newspapers.

The Propaganda and Agitation Section of the central Secretariat has inspectors of its own; their work is largely confined to the supervision of indoctrination, but within this sphere they, too, "jump" over the chain of command by making critical visits not only to the next lower level of Party organization, but to all those below it.

In addition to the Propaganda and Agitation Section, the indoctrination sphere includes the Culture Section, the Science and Educational Institutions Section, and quite possibly the Section for Travel Abroad. All aspects of cultural activity (theaters, radio, television, literature, etc.), science, and education are, in the totalitarian view, closely linked to indoctrination. As will be described in Chapter 5, the aim of the Party is not only to exclude divergent views in all of these intellectual activities, but also to make sure that every medium for the conveyance of ideas is positively attuned to the objectives of the regime. The operational responsibility for attaining this coordination of public expression is assigned to a closely knit body of officials. In the course of his career, an official in this group may occupy such seemingly varied positions as director of a propaganda and agitation section, political adviser to a poetry review, newspaper editor, chairman of a state-television-network committee, and president of a society for the dissemination of atheism. But whatever his job, he is primarily concerned with positive indoctrination. Because of its care in selecting, training, and supervising such officials, the Party can avoid much of the obtrusive and irritating effect of direct censorship, although censorship is always available as a reserve weapon. Instead, the appropriate indoctrination official sees that the Party line is followed by the medium of expression he supervises.

THE PARTY ORGANS SECTION

If any part of the Party apparatus has the potential of acting as the nerve center of the control system, it is the complex known in Western administrative terminology as the "staff agencies." This potential has at times been realized, especially in the period immediately following the Great Purge of 1936–38. At that time, the Cadres Section, charged with the supervision and distribution of personnel, and an Organization-Inspection Section worked closely with the police to maintain the iron, terroristic control of the Party that Stalin required. Malenkov's unpopularity with the Party elite was apparently due in large part to his association with the staff agencies during and after the Great Purge. Since the beginning of World War II, the staff agencies have been reorganized and have somewhat declined in importance. The task of assigning Party personnel to economic fields has been transferred to the various economic ("production-branch") sections of the Secretariat, and to the corresponding sections at lower levels of Party organization. The central Party Organs Section retains the extremely important power of assignment of high- and medium-level personnel to Party and Komsomol organizations as well as to state and trade-union administrative agencies.

The Party Organs sections also play a key role in inspecting the lower Party organizations. As in the case of newspaper "inspection," the chain-of-command concept familiar in Western bureaucracies is frequently disregarded by the Party Organs sections. The central Party Organs Section retains the power of appointment (*nomenklatura*) of some key officials at much lower levels. Similarly, a Party Organs Section inspector from the central Secretariat may unexpectedly visit a district Party organization. As was discussed earlier, assignment of higher Party personnel is a key power at the disposal of the General Secretary. In the 1920's, Stalin ruthlessly utilized the assignment power to reward his adherents and to punish tacitly any official who did not support him: Since all Party members were bound to accept assignments given them by the Secretariat, a recalcitrant official in a key post could be silenced by dispatch on a mission abroad, or tormented by appointment to a post in a remote, undesirable region. Khrushchev used the assignment power much more sparingly, though he did promote a disproportionate number of his followers, especially between 1953 and 1956. It is evident, however, that, in contrast to Stalin, he was unable to "pack" the Central Committee sufficiently to make it his instrument. It is even less likely that the present General Secretary will be able to manipulate assignments enough to establish complete control over the Central Committee. Having rebuffed Khrushchev's attempt to reorganize the apparatus, the Central Committee membership seems to have acquired a consciously autonomous position in the political system. The characteristics of the membership are, consequently, extremely significant.

ELITE SOCIAL CHARACTERISTICS

The Central Committee is composed very largely of high officials of the Party and state bureaucracy. Membership in the Central Committee is, in fact, one of the best criteria we have for assessing the importance of posts in the Soviet bureaucracy. Holders of many important posts are, by custom, virtually ex officio members or alternate members of the Central Committee. Such posts include, of course, the secretaries of the Central Committee. Less certain of election to the Central Committee are directors of Secretariat sections and similar high officials. Together, however, the central Secretariat contingent accounts for about 7 per cent of the current 360 members and alternate members. Union republic first secretaries and first secretaries of most provinces are also almost ex officio holders of Central Committee seats—usually as full members. These territorial Party officials now make up just one-third of the Central Committee, and closely associated state territorial officials constitute 6 per cent more. Central state agencies (a highly fluctuating class in recent years) now provide 25 per cent of the Central Committee—mostly at the candidate level. The military provide 10 per cent of the membership; a scattering come from the diplomatic and from youth and trade-union organizations. A very few are from the arts and sciences or are rank-and-file workers and peasants.

From the educational standpoint, the upper level apparatus (central and territorial Party officials) is divided into three groups. One consists of the indoctrination-machine officials, usually highly trained in ideological exegesis. Another is composed of men (there are very few women at this level) who acquired excellent technical educations—usually in some branch of engineering—before entering the apparatus. A third group, still important though decreasing in numbers, consists of men who entered the apparatus with scanty educations and received practically all their training in Party schools. State officials are almost all men with higher technical education; the disparity between their educational background and that of Party officials from the third group poses a serious problem, for it is difficult for such officials, unsophisticated in technical matters as they are, to supervise those who are equipped to deal with an increasingly complex technology. The problem is likely to be a transient one, however, because engineering training has, for decades, been the key to advancement both in the Party apparatus and in the state system. As noted earlier, the crux of the present problem arises from the resistance of high Party officials, especially at the territorial level, to efforts to replace them with younger, better trained men. Most of the present higher Party officials entered full-time Party service in the 1930's or early 1940's—not long before, or just after, the Great Purge that wiped out the Old Bolsheviks. Their median age level is close to sixty. Of the nine-tenths members of the 1966 Central Committee whose backgrounds can be determined, nearly 80 per cent entered the Party *before* World War II; conversely, less than 5 per cent entered the Party *after* the end of the war. In terms of both age and length of time in the Party, the Central Committee elite presents a striking contrast to the rank-and-file Party members, over half of whom are under forty. The regime has avoided presenting precise data on the length of time the ordinary member has been in the Party, but all indications suggest that an overwhelming majority entered after World War II. The potential for a serious conflict of generations, at least in the sense of psychological difference, exists. During Khrushchev's last years as dictator, the regime seemed to be recognizing this danger by stressing, often deceptively, the rejuvenation of the apparatus. Changes in the Party rules provided for a fixed turnover in many categories of officials. Since Khrushchev's downfall, these rules have been rescinded and the value of long experience is stressed. It is evident, especially in view of the apparent abnormally high incidence of heart disease among the Soviet elite, that the older generation must give way by the early 1970's. In the meantime, one must reckon with the older "men of '38," who went through the trauma of the Great Purge, as the dominant group in the Soviet system.

Elite Attitudes

It is easier to determine the social composition of the Soviet Party and state bureaucracies than it is to gauge their attitudes. It is obvious that the upper strata, at least, occupy a some-

what ambiguous position. On the one hand, they are subject
to severe pressures. Under Stalin, their lives depended on the
caprices of the dictator. The changing interpretations of
Marxism-Leninism mean that they cannot simply follow the
concepts they learned as youths; rather, they have to be ideological acrobats. The system has no use for men who blindly
adhere to the letter of laws or regulations. Reliance upon one's
superior in the chain of command can be dangerous, for channels are often bypassed by the central authorities. These in-
stitutionalized insecurities prod the official to a frantic effort to
prove his loyalty and efficiency. Overfulfillment of assignments
and anticipation of new orders or changes in the Party line are
the best ways to assure one's future. By covert "deals" with
their colleagues to "go easy" on one another, some officials
manage to diminish tensions for a time. Most of the bureaucracy, however, seems to be continually shaken up by the
processes described above. As a result, the procrastinating,
rule-bound Czarist official so familiar to the reader of Russian
classics no longer predominates.

Although the official's life is a tense and strained one, there
are many compensations. Among these, material rewards (relatively high pay, decent living quarters, and the like) are important but probably not dominant. Even when subject to a
dictator, the high Communist official wields power far beyond
that ordinarily exercised by an officer of a modern state, as
the latter is subject to curbs imposed by law and public opinion. Like Lenin (though on a smaller scale), every Soviet
official is an engineer of human society. To a man reared in
a democratic, humanistic tradition, such a role would be repugnant. But the "men of '38" in the Communist apparatus
have come up through a grimmer school. Poor and illiterate
at the advent of the Soviet regime, they owe their positions
and status to that regime.

While the following autobiographical passages are by one

of the relatively uneducated Party leaders (now retired), his attitudes are probably typical of the older group:

I shall tell something about my childhood and youth. I was a foundling. . . . Everybody knew that I was a foundling, and the boys naturally teased me, even though they were afraid of me, for I had a good pair of fists. If not for the Revolution I would have had a bad time of it in my youth. No respectable girl would have married the likes of me—an illegitimate child. . . .

When I was twelve I went to work as a herdsman's helper for a rich farmer in the locality. By fourteen I had left my foster father and begun to live independently. I worked as a herder, horse driver in a mine, and for a building contractor. . . .

I was twenty-three years old but I had no trade, not even any particular goal. Yet one thing I knew, and knew for sure. I would make my way in life. I had a strong body and the army had bred in me a strong will.

I was very eager to study but no technical school or institute would admit me. I did not know enough. I decided, therefore, to go to work and study in my free time. . . .

It was here, on the tunnel job, that I acquired a real working-class schooling and a Bolshevik education. . . .

What were my dreams and aspirations in those days? I was already a grown man, married, and soon father of a baby girl. If anyone had said to me then: now there, Aleksei, think it over— why not aim to go into Party work, to become secretary of a district committee, and then, before you know it, secretary of a regional committee, I would have shrugged my shoulders and laughed. At that time I was not even a Komsomol.

Although I myself was eager to learn, the Soviet Government and the Party were even more eager to have people like me study and develop. . . .

I was elected to the trade union committee and became an active member of the club. On June 27, 1926, I became a candidate member of the Party, and exactly a year later, on June 27, 1927, I was admitted to full Party membership. . . .

[I] had already begun to think of going further, to college, when my life took a different turn. I was called to the city Party committee and told:

"People like you are needed for work in the rural districts."

"What are 'people like me'?"

"Of proletarian origin, reared on the job, devoted to the Party. We haven't enough such people in the rural districts." . . .

The Party continued to keep an eye on me and helped me develop. What theoretical background I lacked was supplied at courses for Party secretaries arranged by the Central Committee in Kiev and subsequently at courses maintained in Moscow by the Central Committee of the CPSU(b).

At the beginning of 1938 I was elected first secretary of the Chernigov Regional Committee of the Communist Party (Bolsheviks) of the Ukraine.*

The official, Aleksei Fyodorov, wrote his memoirs to serve as an example to Communist youth. One may assume that he passes over many a dark aspect of his ascent up the Party ladder during the Purge era. Nevertheless, his faith in the essential rightness of his career seems genuine enough. He started at the bottom of society; through the Party he was able to advance to the top. At the same time, the power of the Soviet Union constantly grew. Quite apart from ideological conviction—which may or may not be deep in men of this type—the correlation between personal advancement on the one hand, and success of the Communist system on the other, must have an enormous psychological impact. Fyodorov implies this himself:

The Soviet person will find nothing particularly novel in my biography. It can be summed up in a few words: I was educated and led forward by the Party, by Soviet power. My mental horizon and my interests broadened hand in hand with the cultural development of the country.†

Increasingly, material success has become the criterion by which the Soviet regime justifies itself—and claims the right to help Communism spread throughout the world. A very

* A. F. Fyodorov, *The Underground R.C. Carries On* (Moscow: Foreign Languages Publishing House, 1952), pp. 33–38.

† *Ibid.,* p. 37.

strong amalgam of self-interest and pride in achievement bind
men like Fyodorov to the Soviet system. As long as they remain
dominant in it, it is hard to see how it can be overturned—
short of some catastrophe of incalculable magnitude—regardless of the personal rivalries and frictions that permeate it:

> I am a full-time Party worker. That means that I devote all my
> time, all my thoughts and all my energies to the Party of Lenin
> and Stalin. And no matter where I am sent, or what I am ordered
> to do by the Party, I carry out the assignment without reservation.
>
> As I look about me now, studying the comrades with whom
> I work shoulder to shoulder, I see that the vast majority of them
> spring from the people. Their life stories are different, but their
> interests and their aims are the same, and these aims are deter-
> mined by the program of the Party of Bolsheviks.*

By 1966, the criterion of material success was shaky. As noted
earlier, failures in agriculture and the crisis over Cuba contributed to Khrushchev's downfall. The split with China has
shown how uncertain are the effects of Communist expansion.
The present generation of Party leaders may retain its faith
in the system, but what of those who, within a decade, must
take their place?

SUGGESTED READING • CHAPTER 4

Nearly all the books on the Soviet system and the Communist
Party listed in the preceding chapter deal with the apparatus. The
following titles deal with particular aspects of the apparatus rather
than Party affairs in general.

ARMSTRONG, JOHN A. *The Soviet Bureaucratic Elite.* New York:
Frederick A. Praeger, 1959. A case study of the backgrounds, turnover, and attitudes of Party officials in the Ukraine.

CONQUEST, ROBERT. *Russia After Khrushchev.* New York: Frederick
A. Praeger, 1965. An examination of rivalries during Khrushchev's
last years in power and an analysis of future prospects.

FAINSOD, MERLE. *Smolensk under Soviet Rule.* Cambridge, Mass.:

* *Ibid.,* p. 38.

Harvard University Press, 1958; Vintage paperback, 1960. Although limited to a single province, this is one of the most important books ever written about the U.S.S.R., because it is based on an extensive file of secret Communist documents originally captured by the German army; these, in turn, were seized by the U.S. forces. All aspects of Soviet life in the 1920's and 1930's are covered, but the revelations on operations of the Party apparatus are especially important.

FYODOROV, ALEKSEI. *The Underground R.C. Carries On.* Moscow: Foreign Languages Publishing House, 1952. Almost the only book of an autobiographical nature by a contemporary high official, this work deals primarily with partisan operations in World War II, but in doing so reveals much concerning the organization and psychology of Party operations.

PISTRAK, LAZAR. *The Grand Tactician.* New York: Frederick A. Praeger, 1961. The best biography of that outstanding *apparatchik* —Khrushchev.

RUSH, MYRON. *Political Succession in the U.S.S.R.* New York: Columbia University Press, 1965. A study of the way top leaders have been replaced.

———. *The Rise of Khrushchev.* Washington, D.C.: Public Affairs Press, 1958. A detailed description of Khrushchev's attainment of power after Stalin's death.

5

INSTRUMENTS OF COERCION

At the beginning of this book, we noted that though political power requires the monopoly of force, force alone is an inadequate basis for a political system. The four chapters that followed showed that the Soviet system is not, in fact, based on force alone. A political culture, the result of a blend of traditional Russian attitudes and totalitarian Communist ideology, is of critical importance. Additionally, the institutional framework of the Communist Party enables a self-chosen and self-perpetuating elite to maintain a monopoly over decision-making. Indoctrination stressing the unique legitimacy of the Party's decisions, inculcation of belief in the inevitability of a perfect Communist social order, almost exclusive control over career advancement, pervasive control of communication channels, are among the powerful factors that maintain this monopoly. Party-elite dominance was not, however, established by these devices. During the first decades of Soviet rule, Lenin and his successors tried to establish total dominance over a society that in large part did not accept the Communist claim to legitimacy. When large elements of a population do not accept a regime's claim to legitimacy, it must either coerce or retreat.

Apart from transient tactical maneuvers, Lenin and all his successors chose to employ force. From the start, the Communists had a strong base of sympathizers in the strategically located urban centers. The regime never neglected persuasion and indoctrination. There is no doubt, however, that without the extensive employment of force, the Soviet regime could not have been stabilized. By the early 1920's, the regime had

achieved a quasi-monopoly of internal force, the usual criterion of an established political system. Until the late 1940's,
however, the Soviet system was subject to more sporadic out-
breaks of armed opposition than are usual in advanced societies. Some, though not all, of these rebellions were encouraged
by the fact that the U.S.S.R. had powerful enemies abroad.
Under these circumstances, the Soviet regime relied in part
on military instruments for maintaining a monopoly of force.

Given the strategic situation of the U.S.S.R., the most important military element has been the ground forces, known
until 1946 as the Red Army and, since then, as the Soviet
Army. The navy has always been distinctly secondary and,
until recent decades, so were the air forces. The army has
been essential in defending the U.S.S.R. in its encounters with
great powers—during the Civil War of 1918–20, in the limited
wars with Japan in 1938–39, and during World War II. The
army has also been the principal means by which the Soviet
regime imposed Communist governments on peripheral areas
of Europe and Asia. Since 1945, the Soviet ground forces have
been the most powerful in the world.

The strength of the Soviet Army and its indispensable services in preserving the Soviet regime have led some observers
to infer that the commanding officers of the military forces
can also dominate the political system. Military commanders
can dominate any society *if* they are determined, as a group,
to do so; if they command the obedience of their troops; and
if they can secure at least passive acquiescence from essential
elements of the civilian population. In other words, the military commanders must establish a considerable measure of
legitimacy in order to govern. A number of factors make attainment of such military legitimacy highly unlikely in the
U.S.S.R.

Communist ideology, with its emphasis on the Party leadership as the sole custodian of doctrinal orthodoxy, is com-

pletely opposed to military rule. It is true that Lenin admired military writers, used military metaphors, and relied on armed force, but he always insisted on complete subordination of the army command. So did his successors, even when, like Stalin, they sought additional prestige by assuming military ranks and uniforms. All Soviet elites, including the military commanders, are composed of Party members indoctrinated in this principle. The other element of the political-cultural amalgam, Russian tradition, also contains no warrant for military rule. Like Stalin, the Czars utilized a military style and military symbols. But, apart from some doubtful cases in early Russian history, no military usurper ever ruled Russia.

This bias against military rule is reinforced by institutional arrangements. During the Civil War, and for two decades afterward, military commanders were required to obtain the countersignature of political officers (commissars) for every order. Since then, the political officers (known at the regimental and divisional levels as deputy directors for political affairs, or *zampolits*) have been more restricted, but they still supervise indoctrination in military units. Political officers have a wide range of personal contacts with rank-and-file soldiers; it is uncertain whether the rank and file would, in case of conflict, obey the military commander or the *zampolit*. The latter is subordinate in strictly military matters to military commanders. At the same time, the *zampolit* has a separate chain of command and reports to the Main Political Administration of the Soviet High Command, which, as noted earlier, is also a section of the Central Committee Secretariat.

The Party leadership has conducted recurrent campaigns against alleged dangers from military coups, opprobriously designated "Bonapartism." The reference is, of course, to Napoleon Bonaparte, who ended the political feuds of the French Revolution by establishing a military dictatorship. In Soviet terminology, the first Bonapartist was Trotsky. Trotsky was, however, no career military officer, though as a Party leader he had been delegated to head the commissar system. Moreover, Trotsky went down to defeat without even trying to use his military connections. In 1937, Stalin accused a group of high military commanders, headed by Marshal Mikhail N. Tukhachevsky, of plotting a coup. In recent years, official Soviet sources have revealed what outside observers long suspected: The "plot" was a frame-up concocted by Stalin. During the early months of the German invasion (1941–42), the Party organization was so demoralized that the military command was compelled to assume many important tasks, but it never tried to seize political power. In 1957, Khrushchev accused the foremost war hero, Marshal Georgi Zhukov, of Bonapartist tendencies and removed him as Minister of Defense. It is true that Zhukov, like many military men, was irritated by tight Party control of the military indoctrination system. It is also true that the military command under his direction had a role, though probably a minor one, in suppressing Beria and the "anti-Party" group. In October, 1957, however, other high officers—among them, Marshal Ivan S. Konev—fiercely criticized Zhukov. Their antagonism indicates that there was never a chance of a united military effort to gain power.

In recent years, the solidity of Party control has been enhanced by delegating a prominent territorial Party official, Aleksei A. Yepishev, to head the Main Political Administration. The chances of a military coup appear even more remote than in the past. It is true, however, that the nature of their recruitment and training makes the army officer corps especially strong in Russian patriotism. If general disillusionment with Communist ideology led to a breakdown of the Soviet political system, it is conceivable that the military command would take power to preserve what they believed to be Russian national interests.

The army was, of course, indispensable to a Soviet victory in the Civil War. Since then, it has rarely been utilized for internal control. Instead, the regime has relied on entirely separate police agencies.* Under Stalin, the police was designed to act as an ultimate safeguard against a military coup as well as against other internal threats. Several divisions, trained and equipped as military formations but completely under police control, were stationed at strategic points such as the environs of Moscow. Soon after Stalin's death and Beria's arrest, these divisions were disbanded. The police organization continues to control sizable military-type formations charged with sealing the Soviet borders against unauthorized passage. These frontier troops formed a special branch of the police organization for decades. In June, 1953, their officers' disaffection for Beria and his security police staff was a prominent factor in the Party leadership's ability to remove Beria.

THE SECURITY POLICE

Under Stalin and Beria, the security police constituted the principal instrument of force for maintaining internal control. The fact that opposition to Stalin's dictatorship could rarely attain the level of armed resistance was largely due to the security police. So pervasive and frightening was its activ-

* The titles of these agencies have changed frequently. At first, the Cheka (Extraordinary Commission) was the core of the police. It was followed by the GPU (State Political Administration), renamed OGPU (Unified State Political Administration) after a few months. Still later, the NKVD (People's Commissariat of Internal Affairs) and the NKGB (People's Commissariat of State Security), at times combined, were the most important police agencies. After 1946, the redesignation of the commissariats as ministries meant that the police agencies' abbreviations became MVD and MGB, respectively. In 1954, the principal central agency became the KGB (Committee on State Security). In 1960, the central MVD was dissolved and, in 1962, Union republic MVD's were redesignated Ministries for Protection of Public Order. The KGB remains as the key central agency controlling both frontier and security police.

ity that many observers identified terror as an essential characteristic of the Soviet political system. Today, terror can hardly be called a permanent characteristic of the system, but it is probable that terror was a necessary means for establishing the system. The principal methods of security-police terror were (1) pervasive clandestine surveillance; (2) secret arbitrary arrest and condemnation; and (3) confinement to concentration camps. By considering each of these methods and its relation to the current Soviet system, one can estimate the extent to which police terror has become obsolete.

Concentration camps have been largely eliminated. At the height of Stalin's dictatorship, fantastic numbers—estimates range from 5 to 20 million—were incarcerated in camps in remote areas of Siberia, Central Asia, and the European Arctic. While systematic brutality seems to have been rare, living conditions in the concentration camps were terrible. Common criminals received better treatment than "politicals." Most prisoners performed arduous physical labor. Clothing and housing were utterly inadequate for the extremely severe climate and hard working conditions. Especially in the years of scarcity during and following World War II, food rations generally were below subsistence levels except for favored categories of prisoners. Even from the purely material standpoint, waste of manpower through the high death rate and through the inherent inefficiency of forced labor was enormous. Almost as soon as Stalin died, the regime began to empty the concentration camps. Apparently, some 80 per cent of the inmates were released by 1956. As described below, there are still corrective labor camps for those who do not adjust to the work requirements of the system. Political prisoners—members of nationalist undergrounds, religious leaders, and dissident intellectuals—still exist. But these categories contain far fewer persons than in 1953.

The present status of security-police surveillance is more

obscure. Under Stalin, the aim was to enfold all of Soviet society in a web of surveillance. For the most part, the professional police director of the "special section" in a military unit, factory, farm, or other element of the Soviet organizational structure relied upon informants outside the police corps. Occasionally these informers were real volunteers, motivated by ideological zeal, patriotic fervor, or personal malice. Soviet indoctrination stressed—and still stresses—the need for universal vigilance against foreign and domestic enemies of the regime. The average citizen, and especially the Party member, is obliged to report suspicious circumstances to the police. There is considerable evidence, however, that many Soviet citizens abhorred the role of informer. In any case, the "special section" directors felt it necessary to recruit a special network of informers bound by formal, though secret, contracts with the police. Many if not most of these contracts were signed under duress. A man accused of crimes was allowed to remain free as long as he informed on his neighbors or fellow-workers; a woman whose husband or father had been sentenced was allowed to send him food parcels as long as she acted as a spy or *agent provocateur*. By one means or another, the police rarely failed to find a professional informer in each critical sector of public life.

The fact that the surveillance network extended even to the Politburo was one reason why the Party elite was eager to curb the security police after Stalin's death. It seems unlikely today that the police dares to maintain regular informers in high Party and government bodies. Soviet sources indicate, however, that the security police still maintains informers among ordinary citizens (such as unauthorized student discussion groups) it suspects. Defectors from the Soviet police and other agencies report that surveillance networks are especially active in aspects of Soviet society related to foreign affairs.

Sweeping personnel changes followed Beria's elimination.

Many of his henchmen were executed; other police leaders were retired within a few years. In 1958, Aleksandr Shelepin, First Secretary of the Communist Youth League, was placed in charge of the KGB. Between 1961 and 1967, another Komsomol secretary, Vladimir Semichastny, held the post; he was followed by Yuri Andropov (who also has a lengthy early background of Komsomol work). Shelepin (as a Party secretary) appears to have continued to supervise the police, which has been assigned many reliable Komsomol members. Stalin also utilized the device of ensuring police loyalty by replacing its officers with Party and Komsomol members. Recent Party leaders, however, have apparently made sure that the police does not become an instrument in the hands of a single official like Shelepin.

Procedural Justice

The third aspect of police terror consisted of secret arrest and arbitrary condemnation after a closed hearing. Arrests were usually made late at night. Families and friends of the arrested person frequently were not informed of his whereabouts for months. During this time, "confessions"—often prepared by the police investigators—were extorted from the accused, both to condemn him and to provide "evidence" against others whom the police wished to incriminate. Interrogations took place in the small hours of the morning, when the prisoner was most susceptible to trickery, psychological pressure, and plain torture. After the confession was secured, the prisoner was brought before a police "special board" empowered to set sentences of up to five years in concentration camps. Apparently, the special boards sometimes even exceeded this legal limit, though death sentences were usually set by secret sessions of military tribunals attached to the regular court system. The special boards operated in complete secrecy. The accused was not informed of the charges until he appeared before the board and was not permitted counsel.

Arbitrary and inhumane as the Soviet security police was in its heyday, it rarely resorted to the public beatings and lynchings that marked Nazi and Fascist police measures. These circumstances did not help the victims, but they did enable the regime to avoid the appearance of barbarity. Moreover, even under Stalin, the vast majority of ordinary crimes (and of legal actions by individuals, which are relatively unimportant under a regime that drastically limits private property) fell under the jurisdiction of a regular judicial system. Very soon after Stalin died, the Soviet regime began to emphasize the judicial system at the expense of the police special boards, which were abolished. To assess the extent of the individual's rights in the U.S.S.R. today, one must, therefore, examine the operations of the judicial system.

The U.S.S.R. (and the Czarist government before it) has always adhered to the Continental European inquisitorial legal system. This system has many advantages for a person accused of an ordinary crime, but it is especially susceptible to abuse when an arbitrary regime considers its interests are at stake. A large part of the administration of justice is in the hands of a procurator who is supposed to carry out completely impartial investigations of crimes, report to the court all circumstances favoring or inculpating the accused, and even appeal cases in which the defendant's rights (as well as the prosecution's) were violated. The Procurator General and his subordinates are officers of a central agency, formally independent of all local judicial, police, and Party authorities. In theory, the procurator can act as a safeguard for the rights of the accused as well as a vigorous defender of the interests of society. Compared to the adversary system prevailing in English-speaking countries, the accused's case is not so heavily dependent upon his ability to engage skillful defense counsel, a condition that can often put poor or ignorant defendants at a severe disadvantage. The accused may retain a defense lawyer of his own choice or be assigned one by the court, but only after the procurator has completed his preliminary investigation. At that point, the accused has the advantage of learning what evidence the prosecution will use against him. However, prior to that point, he may have been held under arrest and interrogated for many weeks while the procurator was building his case. Naturally this case, which is presented in written form to the court, makes a strong impression. Soviet legal authorities insist that, regardless of the conclusion of guilt reached by the procurator during the preliminary investigation, which underlies any case brought to trial, the court must proceed to hear the case without a presumption of guilt. Nevertheless, procurators, and occasionally judges, often appear to be acting on this presumption in court, merely "verifying" the preliminary investigation. The investigation report may contain numerous affidavits by persons who do not appear at the trial, and the accused cannot always have adverse witnesses cross-examined. His defense counsel may be present at the trial but, when state interests appear to be at stake, must act circumspectly. This is especially true in crimes such as espionage, which are tried before the special military tribunal of the U.S.S.R. Supreme Court, where (one suspects) the overriding objective is the accused's abject confession and speedy conviction.

All judges are supposed to give priority to the interests of the state, and the law has always regarded crimes affecting the state as more serious than offenses affecting individuals alone. Nevertheless, the courts constitute a distinct part of the governmental mechanism. Most cases are tried in the "people's courts." Fairly small judicial districts are established for a people's court, but a court may have several judges, with the work being divided on a territorial basis or by types of cases. Judges are nominally chosen by popular election but, as elsewhere in the Soviet electoral system, there is only one nominee, who, in effect, is chosen by the Communist Party. Today, this means that a majority of the judges are professionals, for the Party has insisted on raising the level of legal preparation. As elsewhere in Continental Europe, the judge plays an extremely important role. He may cross-examine the accused and other witnesses at length and freely express his opinion on their testimony. Since hearsay evidence is not prohibited, admissibility of testimony is largely at the judge's discretion. There are no juries. Each case, however, is heard by two "lay assessors," "elected" for two-year terms, who pursue their ordinary occupations except for ten days' court service each year. Nominally, the assessors serving in court have the same powers as the judge and can outvote him on a verdict; in practice, the judge usually guides the decision.

Cases are automatically reviewed by a provincial court, which has original jurisdiction in extremely serious criminal cases; such verdicts are automatically reviewed by the Union Republic Supreme Court. In addition to its original jurisdiction in certain cases such as espionage, the U.S.S.R. Supreme Court reviews some decisions of the lower courts, but (like the U.S. Supreme Court) it usually determines which cases are important enough to merit its attention. All courts include lay assessors when exercising original jurisdiction; reviews are conducted by a panel of professional judges.

SUBSTANTIVE LAW

Though the procedures just described may impress an outside observer as inadequate to safeguard the accused's rights, they were a major aspect of the drive for "socialist legality" after Stalin's death. Another major aspect consisted of sweeping revisions of substantive-law codes. Soviet law has always contained some moderating features, such as the unusual provision that an offender may not be punished for an offense that has ceased to be a "social danger," even if his act was illegal when committed. After Stalin's death, harsh treatment of youthful offenders (who, at the age of twelve, could be punished as adults) was greatly moderated. The step many foreign and Soviet jurists regarded as the greatest substantive achievement of the post-Stalin legal reforms related, significantly, to the definition of crime in general.

One of the most firmly established principles of modern law—older and more widespread than modern democracy—is *nulla poena sine lege:* no penalty except for violation of a specific legal provision. Until 1958, however, Soviet law codes provided that "if one or the other socially dangerous activity is not directly covered by the present Code, the ground and limits of responsibility for it are to be determined in accordance with the articles of the Code covering offenses that resemble it most closely." In 1958, this "principle of analogy" was implicitly repealed by the provision that acts were criminal only if specified by criminal law.

Unfortunately for the individual, the principle of analogy has not been the only vague and sweeping article in the penal codes. At the end of 1961, for example, neglect of farm machinery, even if due to carelessness rather than to intent, was made a crime. Though other provisions (such as the anti-sabotage statute) continue to require intent as an essential element of the crime, the danger that an individual who is merely inept or unlucky may be treated as a criminal still appears to exist. Punishment for the acts of a relative, a clear violation of the principle of individual responsibility, also appears possible at least in marginal cases. Under pre-1958 codes, relatives of a soldier who fled abroad could be exiled to remote areas of the U.S.S.R. for five years even if they had known nothing of the soldier's intentions. This provision was repealed, but, in 1963, a strict Party reprimand was issued to the father of a student who had attempted to cross the frontier illegally (the student himself received a three-year sentence).

The sphere of religious freedom is especially uncertain. As

noted earlier, Communist doctrine is fundamentally atheistic. The whole force of the indoctrination machinery is directed against the "remnants" of religious belief. But all religions are not treated alike. Whatever their motives, the Orthodox Christian bishops, nominally the spiritual guides of most believers in the U.S.S.R., have cooperated with the regime, especially in its "peace" campaigns. In 1962, the late Patriarch Aleksei was even awarded the Order of the Red Banner. The Orthodox Church is very restricted in training priests, using church buildings, and obtaining liturgical books, but it is allowed to function. So are major religious bodies such as Baptists, Lutherans, Latin Catholics, and Moslems. Greek Catholics (see Chapter 6), on the other hand, have been suppressed, and Jews are severely harrassed. So are active small Protestant denominations such as Pentecostalists, Jehovah's Witnesses, and dissident Baptists. Article 124 of the Soviet Constitution cryptically guarantees "freedom of religious worship and freedom of antireligious propaganda." But the law (Article 227 of the R.S.F.S.R. Criminal Code) prohibits both any attempt to persuade others to "abandon public activity" (such as Komsomol membership, where youths are exposed to atheist indoctrination) and any organized religious instruction of young persons. Severe sentences have recently been imposed for organizing Sunday schools. Legally, religious parents may instruct their children at home. In recent years, despite its reaffirmation by jurists, even this freedom has been put in doubt. In 1962, Sergei P. Pavlov, First Secretary of the Communist Youth League, said:

> It must be an object of our special concern to protect children from the influence of believing parents and relatives. The freedom of conscience that is set down in the Constitution applies to adult citizens who can answer for their actions. But we must not allow anyone to cripple a child spiritually, to do violence to his immature mind.*

* *Pravda*, April 17, 1962, as translated in *Current Digest of the Soviet Press*, XIV, No. 16, 5.

About the same time, a father was convicted of "forcing" religion on his daughter, and the children of religious parents were removed to the custody of a brother who had renounced religion.

Church members, like all other Soviet citizens, are strictly forbidden to prepare printed materials or to possess duplicating machines. Furthermore, Article 70 of the R.S.F.S.R. Criminal Code (and corresponding articles in other republic codes) forbids all "agitation or propaganda conducted in order to undermine or weaken the Soviet power . . . or even distribution, preparation, or possession for the same purpose of literature of such content." This provision is so vague that anyone critical of any fundamental aspect of the Soviet system can be condemned. In 1960, several men were put on trial for operating an "underground publishing house" issuing prayer books; about the same time, a Swedish seaman was apprehended "smuggling" Bibles into Leningrad.

Until very recently, it seemed possible that the rigorous penalties for anti-Soviet propaganda would be applied only to religious or underground nationalist organizations. In 1965, however, a young British teacher was sentenced to five years' imprisonment for the sole offense of distributing leaflets prepared by an émigré organization. The following year, two well-known Soviet writers, Andrei Sinyavsky and Yuli Daniel, were sentenced to long prison terms for violation of Article 70 alone. While their writings, published abroad under pseudonyms, undoubtedly satirized Soviet life, the authors vainly denied any intention of "undermining Soviet power."

Sinyavsky and Daniel were directly accused of anti-Soviet propaganda and given a formally correct, if summary trial. In some respects this action is gratifying, because it means that the regime openly admits its severe limitation of intellectual freedom. Usually, the Soviet leadership proceeds to suppress opposition by more devious means. As indicated earlier, the regime's monopoly of all publishing facilities enables it to suppress most public criticism at the source. The most distinguished predecessor of Sinyavsky and Daniel who evaded this prohibition by publishing abroad was Boris Pasternak. When his novel, *Dr. Zhivago,* won a Nobel Prize, he was not punished directly; instead, he was warned that he would not be allowed to return to the U.S.S.R. if he went abroad to receive the award. After Pasternak's death, his companion and her daughter were imprisoned, ostensibly for currency violations. Even more devious has been the practice, used in more than a dozen cases in recent years, of confining offending authors in mental hospitals.

SOCIAL DISCIPLINE MEASURES

The tendency of even the post-Stalin Soviet regime to utilize vague, catch-all decrees rather than precise criminal law is equally apparent in enforcement of "social discipline." Under Stalin, every worker was *legally* bound to his job; changes could take place only with the permission of management. Absence or even tardiness was a criminal offense, although the penalties were eased in the last years of Stalin's life. Probably no single aspect of the Soviet system was more bitterly resented by the common man. The labor discipline laws were, therefore, abolished in 1956. But many restrictions on freedom of movement remain. Unauthorized job changes can cost a worker his social-security benefits. Every Soviet citizen must carry a domestic passport and report every change of residence to the police. Transportation to another locality is often hard to obtain unless one has an official requisition. The police are authorized to expel "loafers" from many of the most important (and attractive) cities. Graduates of universities and other higher educational institutions are legally bound to work at assigned jobs for several years. Party members must accept job assignments on penalty of expulsion.

But all of these restrictions, it seems, have not been able to ensure the complete devotion to work demanded by the feverish tempo of Soviet economic development. Even with considerable increase in the availability of consumers' goods, incentive pay is inadequate to induce all workers to devote their full capacities to production. Attempts to gain money by using state property or by speculating (buying and selling for a profit) have been criminal for decades. In recent years, those who resort to large-scale theft of state property or currency speculation have been condemned to death—a far harsher punishment than is meted out for property crimes in capitalist societies. By 1958, the Soviet regime evidently was also determined to punish those it suspected of living off illegal earnings—without bothering to prove that they had actually engaged in embezzlement or speculation—and to suppress loafing and other violations of work discipline even if the offender had no illegal earnings. Coupled with this immediate purpose was the regime's long-range intention, under Khrushchev, to move from legal enforcement toward "social persuasion." The 1961 Party program, and the statements that preceded it, regarded such a move as an essential step on the way to Communism. Social persuasion would enable the state and its instruments of law and coercion to "wither away." At the same time, social persuasion would act as an educational device to prepare Soviet citizens for the stage when each would work "according to his ability" without regard for reward or punishment.

One technique of social persuasion, the Komsomol youth patrols, has already been mentioned. Another, also still in operation, is the "comrades' court." These bodies, set up at places of work and in residences, consist of several laymen nominally chosen by trade unions or local governmental bodies, but, in all likelihood, actually appointed by the Party. They may deal with a wide range of minor offenses, whether strictly illegal or not: drunkenness, neglect of one's family, absenteeism, poor-quality work, carelessness. Since comrades' courts act without concern for the rules of legal procedure, they obviously violate the principle of "socialist legality." Because the punishments they may impose are slight (public reprimands, fines, job demotions), this violation did not at first seem crucial. In 1958, however, decrees issued in the Central Asian republics authorized "popular assemblies" to banish offenders against work discipline. Soviet jurists protested strongly. Nevertheless, in 1961, a similar decree was issued for the R.S.F.S.R. "Working-people's collectives" were empowered to punish anyone "in actual fact undermining discipline or labor, engaging in private enterprise, living on funds obtained by nonlabor means, or committing other antisocial acts that enable them to lead a parasitic way of life." Authorized punishment was five years' compulsory work in an enterprise in a specified place of banishment. Administration was, as under Stalin, very much in the hands of the police, who carried out the investigation, met the "delinquent" at his place of banishment, and confined him to a "corrective-labor camp" if he failed to make good at his assigned job.

Many observers expected that the popular assemblies or collectives might become a major extra-legal instrument of coercion. In fact, however, the regime seems to have resorted to an alternative method provided in the decree—hearings by a regular people's court. Even under Khrushchev, the emphasis on instruments of social persuasion, including the comrades' courts, appears to have been more verbal than practical. Since his ouster, the regime has evidently quietly downgraded these, like other aspects of the 1961 program. In September, 1965, the "parasite" decree for the R.S.F.S.R. was revised. All penalties and proscriptions were retained, but references to workers' collectives were deleted, leaving proceedings to the people's courts and to local governmental bodies.

Downgrading the "popular" techniques for enforcing social

persuasion means that a Soviet citizen accused of a serious offense will appear before a regularly constituted court. Its proceedings can be summary enough; in one case, a woman was sentenced to five years' banishment after a hearing of five minutes. Witnesses who have no personal knowledge of the offense play a prominent role in expressing "public opinion" against the accused "parasite." "Antiparasite" procedures are especially ominous when the accused is someone the regime suspects of intellectual unreliability. Together with the devices for suppressing the intellectual that were discussed earlier, the "parasite" decrees narrowly constrict the range of individual freedom in the U.S.S.R.

The Soviet system can no longer be called a police state in the usual sense of the term. High police officials do not exert major influence on policy decisions and the police as an institution is not a major factor in political struggles. Terror, in the sense of wholesale punishment for political offenses, is ended, at least for the time being. The memory of the terror that lasted until 1953 will not vanish until the present generation of Soviet citizens has gone its way. Undoubtedly, the fears this memory inspires serve as a subtle reinforcement for the indirect means of intellectual control and social discipline the regime prefers to employ. In crucial cases, however, the regime has demonstrated that it will resort to harsh measures, using instruments of surveillance and coercion different only in degree from Stalin's.

SUGGESTED READING • CHAPTER 5

Many of the books listed in chapters 3 and 4 contain detailed discussions of the police system in the context of Soviet political developments. The only major work specifically devoted to the police system, however, is *The Soviet Secret Police,* edited by Simon Wolin and Robert M. Slusser (New York: Frederick A. Praeger, 1957), based on émigré accounts and on analyses of Soviet publications.

Most of the numerous accounts by defectors from the Soviet police and intelligence networks are so lurid that they are hard for the nonspecialist to evaluate intelligently, but Walter Krivitsky's *I Was Stalin's Agent* (London: Hamish Hamilton, 1939), though dated, is still remarkably good. Three books on purges and the treatment of prisoners (in the Stalin era) stand out:

BECK, F., and GODIN, W. *Russian Purge and the Extraction of Confession*. London: Hurst and Blackett, 1951. A remarkably dispassionate analysis by two purge victims.

BRZEZINSKI, ZBIGNIEW. *The Permanent Purge*. Cambridge, Mass.: Harvard University Press, 1955. A scholarly study of the Great Purge of 1936–38, and of the general implications of the purge process.

LEITES, NATHAN, and BERNAUT, ELSA. *The Ritual of Liquidation*. Chicago: The Free Press of Glencoe, 1954. A debatable but very interesting interpretation of the motivation and procedure of the Great Purge.

Among the many personal accounts of the imposition of controls on Soviet cultural life, Juri Jelagin's *Taming of the Arts* (New York: Dutton & Company, 1951) stands out. On legal theory, Towster's book listed in Chapter 3, is especially useful, as are the following specialized works:

BERMAN, HAROLD J. *Justice in the U.S.S.R*. Rev. ed. Cambridge, Mass.: Harvard University Press; and New York: Vintage paperback, 1963. A competent account by a lawyer specializing in the Soviet legal system.

HAZARD, JOHN N. *Law and Social Change in the USSR*. London: Stevens & Sons, 1953. A lawyer and political scientist who combines American and Soviet legal training. Hazard is pre-eminently qualified to analyze this topic.

A book of capital importance, but hard to place in any special category because it is essentially an analysis (based on very extensive interviewing of émigrés) of the reactions of the Soviet people to its regime is

INKELES, ALEX, and BAUER, RAYMOND A. *The Soviet Citizen*. Cambridge, Mass.: Harvard University Press, 1959.

6

THE SOVIETS
AND THE NATIONALITIES

At first glance it seems anomalous that one can examine a wide range of fundamental Soviet political institutions before considering the formal constitution of the country. As has already been described, however, the real locus of power is the Party, not the formal governmental structure; and even certain crucial elements nominally within that structure, like the police, have had little relation to the constitutional prescriptions. Indeed, it is often asked why the U.S.S.R. has a constitution providing for a formal governmental system at all. One reason, certainly, is the burning nationality question, outlined later in this chapter. Another is the need to impress the outside world and the Soviet people with the claim that the Soviet state is the "most democratic in the world." Aside from these motivations, however, Communist ideology has constantly proclaimed the necessity of distinguishing (before complete Communism is attained) between the Party, supreme though its decision-making power be, and the detailed legislative and administrative tasks that must be performed by the state. Maintenance of a separate state structure serves the additional function of drawing large numbers of Soviet citizens into the operation of the system, without the necessity of diluting the Party ranks with unacceptable human material. The Soviet state is indeed a façade behind which the real power of Communist control is exercised, but it is a façade that is not wholly devoid of functional significance.

THE SOVIETS

Lenin sharply criticized parliamentary government as a screen, "the most perfect shell" (because the most deceptive) for rule by the capitalists. Existing legislative bodies were "bourgeois talk shops," which could not be utilized for the "dictatorship of the proletariat" even after complete overhauling. Today, when Communist ideologues write of the "parliamentary path to socialism" (see Chapter 2), they envisage parliaments only as avenues for Communist seizure of power, not as permanent legislatures in Communist states. However, since Lenin, like his followers, insisted on a state structure apart from the revolutionary Party, he needed a new form of legislative body. He found it in the "soviets." The original soviets were merely *ad hoc* bodies ("soviet" means simply "council" in Russian) formed by worker groups to direct the general strike at the start of the unsuccessful 1905 Revolution. Lenin's Bolsheviks neither originated nor dominated these soviets, but he welcomed them as a proletarian creation that, unlike parliaments, combined execution with deliberation. Doubtless Lenin was also aware that the impetuous nature of the soviets and their lack of procedural rules and traditions would make them easier for a conspiratorial minority to manipulate. When the soviets were revived during the 1917 Revolution, the Bolsheviks, with their temporary Left Social Revolutionary allies, eventually did succeed in dominating the soviets, which were then adopted as the symbol of the Bolshevik regime.

THE CONSTITUTION

Soviets in the present-day U.S.S.R. are rather different, however, from the original bodies composed of delegates from factories, railroad lines, and military units. In 1936, a new constitution was adopted as part of Stalin's plan for strengthening and regularizing the state structure and at the same time making it superficially more attractive to world democratic opinion.* On the ground that hostile classes no longer existed in the Soviet Union (industrial workers, peasants, and "intelligentsia" all qualified as "toilers"), all citizens over eighteen not detained in concentration camps were declared entitled to equal and direct vote for members of the legislative bodies. Consequently, instead of being elected from occupational bodies, soviet deputies are elected, as in most Western countries, from territorial districts. The highest level, the Supreme Soviet of the U.S.S.R., consists of the Council of the Union, composed of over 700 members elected from single-member districts with a population of approximately 300,000 each, and the Council of Nationalities, composed of somewhat fewer deputies apportioned among the nationality subdivisions outlined below, with the deputies elected at large. The Supreme Soviet is, therefore, a bicameral body. But many of its most important sessions are held jointly.

The Supreme Soviet is elected for a four-year term (in even-numbered years other than leap years—1962, 1966, etc.—since there was a hiatus during the war period). The voter turnout (about 99.9 per cent) is startling, until one notes the tremendous effort and pressure brought to bear by the regime to secure universal participation. Indeed, the principal function of a Soviet election is obviously that of a mass rally in favor of the regime rather than an exercise of popular sovereignty. The ballots have never listed more than one nominee per office. Numerous accounts make it evident that the Party picks the nominees in advance. Even Article 141 of the Constitution

---

* Plans for a revised constitution have been discussed for several years, but, at present, it is hard to tell whether the regime is seriously planning a change.

hints at this situation by listing the Party first among "public organizations and societies of the working people" entitled to nominate, while Article 126 states that "the most active and politically conscious citizens in the ranks of the working class and other sections of the working people unite in the Communist Party . . . which . . . is the leading core of all organizations of the working people, both public and state." A recent Soviet article puts the matter bluntly:

During the nomination of candidates for Deputy many meetings name several candidates. Why does only one candidate's name remain on the ballot? Back in 1937, M. I. Kalinin, speaking at the pre-election rally in Leningrad, said: "If in our country in a number of places candidates withdraw their names in favor of a single candidate, this is the consequence of their social kinship and the community of their political goals. After thorough discussion, tens and thousands of voters have agreed on a single candidate. This is also a hallmark of socialism, a sign that there is no, and cannot be any, discord among our laboring masses, the kind of inner discord that exists within bourgeois society." . . . This is why all Soviet people have recognized the Communist Party as the guiding force of our society, the directing nucleus of all state and public organizations. This is written in Article 126 of the U.S.S.R. Constitution, the basic law of our state. This is why our Party, Y.C.L., trade union and other public organizations, all the working people come forward at elections in a single bloc—the bloc of Communists and non-Party people. This is why in our country all the voters unanimously cast their ballots for the candidates of this bloc, as the best and most worthy representatives of the people.*

Aside from its determination to fill the Supreme Soviet (and all other soviets) with reliable deputies, the Party maintains complete direction of nominations in order to form the Soviet version of the "balanced ticket." Supreme Soviet delegations from each major area are carefully arranged to include repre-

---

* P. Tumanov, "Guarantees of Democratism," *Izvestia*, May 13, 1966, as translated in *Current Digest of the Soviet Press*, XVIII, No. 19, 32–33.

sentatives of the nationality groups, various occupational categories, and women. In addition, persons who are celebrities —war heroes, exemplary workers, and (probably less often) cultural figures—often appear on the ballots. Such slates serve two purposes: They give each major population group a feeling that it is represented, however little the nominee may really have in common with this particular group; and they suggest that all outstanding citizens are lined up behind the regime.

Thus the Soviet electoral campaign assumes the aspect of an affirmation of solidarity in support of the Communist system. Frequently it is also the occasion for stressing some particular propaganda line of the moment. Obviously, in addition to a complete voter turnout there must be a virtually unanimous vote for the nominees, who symbolize solidarity. There is. All unmarked ballots cast are counted in favor of the uncontested nominees; consequently, there is no need for the voter to exercise his constitutional right of retiring to a private polling booth *unless he wishes to oppose the ticket.* Foreign observers at recent elections report that extremely few voters are bold enough to do this. In a very small number of local elections, individual nominees have been rejected when a majority of the voters crossed out their names. Whether these instances were prearranged or whether they represented a spontaneous rejection of very unpopular persons whom the Party is willing to see discarded is not known.

LEGISLATIVE PROCEDURE

According to the Constitution, the Supreme Soviet is the primary legislative body of the U.S.S.R. But an examination of its operation indicates that the Supreme Soviet could not really consider much legislation even if its members were able and willing to make fundamental political decisions. The Constitution provides for semiannual sessions; these have in fact been held since Stalin's death. Each session is very short, however—usually it lasts less than a week. These sessions seem like mere ceremonies of ratification, characterized by set speeches rather than debate, and by unanimous acceptance of legislation introduced by government spokesmen. Since the Supreme Soviet members have regular jobs apart from their legislative duties, it is obvious that they lack both the time and the sustained familiarity with governmental business needed to exercise real influence on legislative proposals. It is true that various standing commissions (committees) of the houses of the Supreme Soviet review these proposals in advance of the sessions. Much of these commissions' operations is obscure, since their deliberations are not described in detail in the Soviet press. Recently, the commissions seem to have become somewhat more active. It appears that a proposal receives somewhat more detailed consideration in the commission than in the Supreme Soviet as a whole, but that the commission's deliberations are guided by its carefully selected Party contingent. In recent years, public discussions of specific features of a few items of proposed legislation have taken place. The reorganization of industrial direction considered in the spring of 1957 is an example of such discussion. The participation of members of the commissions considering the legislation in such press debates suggests that commission consideration may in fact proceed before the final form of the proposed law is decided. Such discussion takes place only when authorized (either because of real policy indecision or for tactical reasons) by the Party leadership. In the case of industrial reorganization, Khrushchev's report on the "theses of the Central Committee and the Council of Ministers" that preceded the press discussion was couched in language clearly designed to indicate that the details of reorganization were open to discussion. More often, however, a firm decision is made by a Party meeting (Central Committee meetings frequently take place just before the Supreme Soviet convenes) and is merely ratified by the nominal legislative body. For example, in its plenary session of January, 1955, the Central Committee secretly decided to replace Malenkov as prime minister; his resignation, presented to the Supreme Soviet session early in February, was just a formality.

In spite of its docility, the Supreme Soviet is not always permitted to exercise even the formal power of passing the legislation the Constitution assigns to its sphere. Many major laws are in fact enacted as decrees of the Presidium of the Supreme Soviet. This body of thirty-three members nominally elected by the Supreme Soviet in joint session can be manipulated more readily than the entire legislative body. Actually in session, or available, at all times, the Presidium is the formal collective head of state of the U.S.S.R. Its chairman (at present, N. V. Podgorny) acts as the formal representative of the Soviet state in dealing with foreign emissaries. Many of the laws are initially issued as decrees of the Presidium or of the Council of Ministers. Many are later perfunctorily ratified by the Supreme Soviet, but other decrees on a wide variety of subjects remain in force without even this nominal ratification.

In view of all these circumstances, it is no exaggeration to describe the Supreme Soviet not as a real legislature but as a rubber stamp. In line with Lenin's concept of the soviets as working bodies, however, Communist writers claim another substantial function for the Supreme Soviet—that of overseeing the administration of the laws. But there is no evidence that the Supreme Soviet actually performs this function. Except for the limited commission activity, there is no institutional arrangement to facilitate legislative oversight, such as the question period in the British House of Commons or the committee investigation of the American Congress. One may well ask, therefore, what the real purpose of the Supreme Soviet is. As noted above, it impresses some segments of world opinion with the "democratic content" of the Soviet system. Its elections and its sessions serve as demonstrative rallies of opinion behind the regime. In addition, Supreme Soviet sessions may be viewed as "schools" for impressing the relatively humble and provincial figures who constitute much (though by no means all) of its membership with the nature of the current Party line and the potency of the Soviet system. The deputies, in turn, transmit these concepts to their remote constituents. Deputies who learn their lesson exceptionally well may be drawn into the Party apparatus itself. Thus, Supreme Soviet sessions (and especially those of local soviets) may serve as part of the cadres screening process. Furthermore (following Lenin's view of the soviets as barometers), the Party utilizes the Supreme Soviet sessions as a device for testing public opinion. This is accomplished not through the "dangerous" procedures of uncontrolled debate and voting, but by more indirect sounding of the attitudes of deputies who, after all, have been chosen to represent to some degree the extremely varied geographical, national, and social groups of the U.S.S.R. Finally, the Supreme Soviet must necessarily exist as a cap to the whole system of state elective bodies.

LOCAL SOVIETS

Immediately below the Supreme Soviet are the supreme soviets of the Union republics; their significance is noted later in this chapter. Leaving aside other nationality divisions, the next-lower level of the administration is usually the province (oblast), of which there are approximately 120. Each province has a soviet elected from single-member territorial districts for a two-year term. In contrast to the U.S.S.R. arrangement, the provincial soviet has no presidium or council of ministers, but an executive committee, which combines the functions of both at a lower level. Similarly, the 1,600 city and the 3,000 district

FORMAL STRUCTURE OF THE SOVIET GOVERNMENT

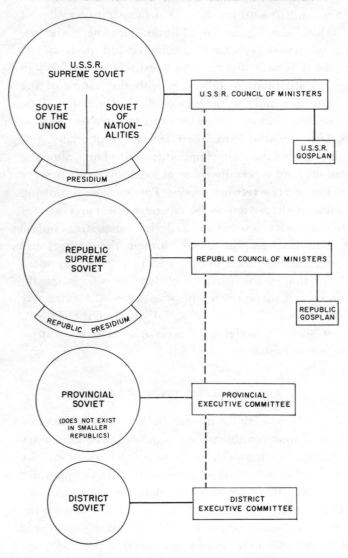

(rayon) soviets (elected in the same way) have only executive committees. However, in larger local areas, the presidium of the executive committee seems to carry out most of the duties nominally assigned to the executive committee. The lowest territorial subdivision, the village (about 49,000 in number), usually has only a chairman, vice-chairman, and a secretary. Even Soviet sources admit that the practical importance of the village soviet and its officers is negligible.

Sessions of the local soviets at all levels tend to be perfunctory ceremonies. In one respect, however, especially in cities, the soviet—within its own area—may have an importance much greater than that of the Supreme Soviet. The principal distinguishing feature is the importance of the standing commissions of the soviet. Since their constituencies are small, members of local soviets (even though they owe their election to Party manipulation) are more immediately and practically concerned with the needs of the people whom they nominally represent. Assignment of deputies to local soviet commissions is usually based on practical qualifications: e.g., a teacher or a mother may be assigned to the educational commission. Here the deputy may play a role of real, if limited, importance. He cannot alter or even criticize basic policies of the regime. He can, however, serve as a channel for criticism and suggestions from constituents whose interests and background are not very different from his own, and his own special experiences qualify him to deal with considerable assurance with the problems that confront his commission. Deputies serving on a commission may be given reduced schedules in their usual jobs. The deputies are then able to devote considerable time to on-the-spot inspection of the local administrative agency with which the commission is concerned. Sometimes the deputies even provide practical assistance for the agencies. This activity tends not only to be functionally useful, but also tends to "humanize" the Soviet system at this level by bringing it in contact with ordinary people and their problems. In a sense, it may even give an impression of "grass-roots" democracy to constituents who secure practical relief as a result of their complaints to their deputies. But both constituents and deputy are aware that the range of safe complaints is limited.

THE SOVIET EXECUTIVE

Basic decisions made by the Party apply to the executive or administrative arm of the Soviet Government as well as the legislative branch, but administrative operations have considerably greater importance than legislative operations do. Under Stalin, various aspects of the government administration tended to assume positions in the power structure (under the absolute dictator) on a par with the Party. This was particularly true of the police machine and, during World War II, the military forces. But Stalin also tended to elevate the position of the directing body of the government administration, the Council of Ministers. For more than a decade prior to his death, Stalin held the position of head of government (Chairman of the Council of Ministers, generally called Premier) as well as head of the Party (General Secretary). After Stalin died, Georgi Malenkov surrendered his Party Secretaryship shortly after assuming the post of Premier; yet, for months, he seemed to be the most powerful figure in Soviet politics. Khrushchev's ascendancy meant a restoration of Party supremacy. The Council of Ministers remained somewhat important, however, as indicated by Khrushchev's assumption of the Premiership in 1958. Since Khrushchev's ouster, the Premiership has again been held by a leader (Aleksei N. Kosygin) who is not simultaneously Party chief, and the Council of Ministers has regained significance.

As was noted above, the Council of Ministers is the directing agency of the executive branch of the Soviet Government.

While the Party makes the basic decisions, the Council of Ministers plays a very important role in carrying them out, issuing decrees with the force of law that in fact constitute much of the important legislation of the U.S.S.R. Just below the Chairman, or Premier, are two First Deputy Chairmen and nine Deputy Chairmen. Each of these apparently supervises a specific sphere of governmental activity. In addition, the Chairman and Deputy Chairmen constitute a kind of inner cabinet of the Council of Ministers. The Council itself includes, in addition to the chairmen just described, about fifty ministers and a dozen heads of committees and similar bodies. Chairmen of Union-Republic councils of ministers are also at least nominal members of the U.S.S.R. Council of Ministers. Among the important bodies represented there, the People's Control Committee deserves special mention because it serves as the "staff agency" for internal inspection of the government bureaucracy. The presence in the Council of Ministers of the directors of so many bodies, in addition to the heads of the other ministries, means that the Council continues to be an unwieldy body requiring direction by the smaller group of Chairman and Deputy Chairmen.

The Ministries

There are two types of central ministries: All-Union and Union-Republic. All-Union ministries direct matters exclusively in the sphere of central government; consequently, these ministries are found only in Moscow. Most of the All-Union ministries direct major branches of the economy. Union-Republic ministries, on the other hand, direct spheres of activities, that, at least nominally, are shared by the central government and the Union republics.* Consequently, in addition to

* A few of the state committees of ministerial level are also legally organized as Union-Republic agencies.

the ministers in Moscow, who are members of the Council of Ministers of the U.S.S.R., there are counterpart ministers in some or all of the Republic capitals. In Soviet legal theory, the Union-Republic ministries in republic capitals are subordinate both to the corresponding Union-Republic minister in Moscow and to the council of ministers of the republic. If it were not for the peculiar nature of the Soviet system, it is hard to see how this dual subordination could operate smoothly; but in practice, both the Moscow Union-Republic minister and his counterparts in the republics must follow Party decisions. In addition, the Soviet Constitution provides that a "definite and limited number" of agencies in the sphere of a Union-Republic ministry may be directed exclusively by Moscow. In the case of the Ministry of Defense (nominally Union-Republic), apparently all activity is directed by the Minister in Moscow. For many years, as a matter of fact, the identity of none of the ministers of defense in the republic capitals has been revealed. In practice, the conduct of foreign affairs is equally centralized. It is true that the republics have counterpart ministries of foreign affairs, but these are merely propaganda agencies designed to deal with foreign visitors and send delegations to international organizations. Though nominally a Union-Republic ministry, the Ministry of Foreign Affairs in Moscow is the sole governmental authority for the conduct of diplomatic relations. The central ministries maintain a very large measure of control in other areas as well; for example, they require adherence to uniform study plans in the higher educational institutions.

As the preceding discussion indicates, each of the fifteen Union republics has its own council of ministers.* Like the central Council of Ministers, each of the republic councils is

---

* The R.S.F.S.R. has its own council of ministers (in Moscow) as well as its own supreme soviet, even though (as noted in Chapter 3) it does not have a Party organization like that of the other republics.

headed by a chairman (at present none of these are Party secretaries), assisted by several first deputy chairmen and deputy chairmen. Each republic council of ministers also contains a number of committees and commissions, including, in particular, counterparts of the State Planning Committee and the People's Control Committee. The republic councils of ministers also comprise, of course, the republic counterparts of the Union-Republic ministries in Moscow, though some republics do not have all of these ministries. In addition, each republic has a number of ministries for which there are no Moscow counterparts. As a rule, these are ministries for motor transport and highways; municipal utilities; education; social security; construction; local industry; and protection of public order. In theory, these ministries operate without direct control from Moscow; in practice, their activities are closely coordinated and supervised by various central governmental and Party agencies. In particular, this holds true for the republic ministries for protection of public order, which are under the close supervision of the central Committee on State Security (KGB). The activities of the republic ministries probably have some administrative advantages, inasmuch as they provide a measure of decentralization in the huge Soviet Union. The presence of the councils of ministers in the republic capitals also provides a semblance of independence for the republics. But the power to decide important matters remains firmly lodged in the central apparatus in Moscow.

LOCAL EXECUTIVE BODIES

The executive bodies in the provinces, districts, and cities are less complicated than those at the republic level.* Each of these levels of government generally has departments that are

* The autonomous republics (A.S.S.R.'s) have councils of ministers resembling (on a smaller scale) those of the Union republics.

branches of the republic ministries and that work under ministry direction. Each local level also has an executive committee elected by the soviet of the area. The executive committee exercises general supervision of administration and at the same time functions as an interim legislative body, since the local soviets do not elect presidiums empowered to act between sessions of the soviets.

The Functional Position of the Nationalities In Soviet Policy

A survey of the general situation of nationalities in the U.S.S.R. is hardly enough to reveal the vital role they play in the Soviet system; there is little doubt that the regime actually has quite different aims for individual national groups. Borrowing a term used in a different context to describe social organizations, we may conclude that each nationality has a special "function" from the standpoint of the regime's objectives. The regime does not openly avow these aims, but they can be deduced, with a reasonable degree of certainty, by piecing together scattered evidence. Most of this evidence is derived from examining the history of Soviet policy toward individual nationalities and from reading between the lines of Soviet policy statements. In contrast to most aspects of the Soviet political system, there is a considerable body of statistical data concerning the nationalities. Manipulation of this statistical data enables one to construct "indicators" of several crucial elements of the nationality situation. One group of indicators, as listed in the Nationalities Table (pages 142–43) in this chapter, provides additional though indirect evidence on Soviet aims.*

* The statistics that form the basis for calculating the indicators are drawn from numerous Soviet sources. The most important source is the 1959 census (which is the base for population and linguistic calculations), but a large number of statistical handbooks for various subsequent years have also been used. Consequently, data are not always exactly compar-

Since Party membership is controlled by Moscow, the proportion of Party members of each nationality tends to reflect the extent to which the regime emphasizes the integration of that nationality into the dominant political element. Central Committee membership is an even stronger indication of political integration. One must be careful to note, however, that both these indicators are only suggestive of trends; factors other than the regime's objectives may influence the statistics. This reservation applies even more strongly to the other indicators of Soviet policy. In large measure, the proportion of Russians residing in the home territory of each nationality reflects deliberate Soviet encouragement of migration since 1917, but to some extent the migration of Russians to these areas has been voluntary, or occurred before the Revolution. Similarly, the proportions of printed materials issued, while ultimately subject to the regime's control, are also influenced by popular demand in each nationality group. Consequently, only by examining a combination of these indicators, together with the historical evidence and Soviet policy statements, can one draw conclusions concerning the nature of Soviet objectives. We shall follow this procedure in discussing each nationality.

Indicators of social mobilization are somewhat less ambiguous. Social mobilization is the process by which a basically agricultural society with a traditional culture becomes "modernized," that is, comes to resemble the urban industrial societies of Western Europe and the United States. As noted in Chapter 2, a major objective of the Soviet regime has been modernization along these lines. Consequently, the functions performed for the regime by each nationality are closely re-

able, and, in some instances, approximate estimates had to be used. In order to avoid conveying a spurious impression of accuracy, most indicators have been rounded off. For a more detailed analysis, see my article "The Ethnic Scene in the Soviet Union—the View of the Dictatorship," in *Ethnic Minorities in the Soviet Union,* ed. Erich Goldhagen (New York: Frederick A. Praeger, 1967).

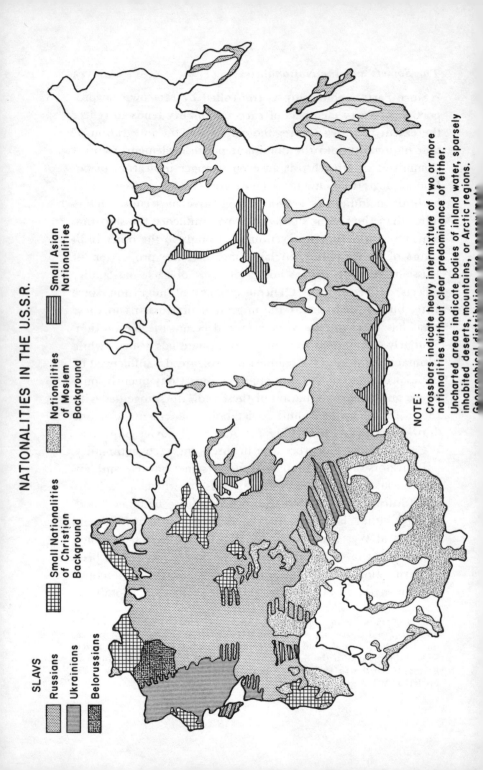

NATIONALITIES IN THE U.S.S.R.

SLAVS

▨ Russians

▦ Ukrainians

▧ Belorussians

▨ Small Nationalities of Christian Background

▨ Nationalities of Moslem Background

▥ Small Asian Nationalities

NOTE:

Crossbars indicate heavy intermixture of two or more nationalities without clear predominance of either.

Uncharted areas indicate bodies of inland water, sparsely inhabited deserts, mountains, or Arctic regions.

Geographical distributions are approximate.

lated to the nationality's degree of social mobilization. The proportion of urban inhabitants is, by definition, an indicator of social mobilization. Experience throughout the world indicates that birth rates are also a very important indicator: They are high in traditional and transitional societies, lower in fully modernized societies. Unfortunately, data on birth rates of Soviet nationalities are very incomplete.* However, because infant mortality is very low throughout the U.S.S.R., data on the proportion of each nationality below age twenty provide a fairly satisfactory supplementary indicator. Most traditional societies place a much lower value on the education of girls than of boys; hence, the relationship between the proportions of males and females with more than the legally required elementary education is also a good indicator of social mobilization. Indeed, all indicators of relative educational achievements are also indicators of the extent of social mobilization. Since virtually all people in the U.S.S.R. receive elementary educations, simple criteria such as the extent of literacy (frequently used to compare developing nations) are worthless in comparing Soviet nationalities. Examination of higher educational achievement is meaningful, and several indicators of such achievement are given in the Nationalities Table. One must be cautious in using these indicators, however, for some (particularly current enrollments in higher education) may reflect artificial stimulation of the educational level by the regime rather than long-term educational achievement by the nationality group. Another major indicator of social mobilization is the extent to which members of a group change their place of residence, though this factor may also be influenced by the regime's decisions. Data for nationality groups as a whole are unavailable, but data on two select groups do provide some basis for comparison of residential mobility. The extent to which students leave their own nationality area to study in the Russian Re-

* The available data have been assembled by Karl-Eugen Waedekin in *Osteuropa*, 1964, No. 11, p. 839.

public is one; the extent to which scientists leave to work in the R.S.F.S.R. is another. The available statistics do not enable one to determine the precise proportions of these groups (some of each group now residing in the R.S.F.S.R. were born there), but the data provide at least crude indicators of residential mobility.

Finally, there are indicators of the extent to which each nationality has become Russified. In a sense, these indicators represent the "feedback" of Soviet policy for Russification is a general objective. However, the indicators do provide evidence of Soviet policy intentions: The relative success in Russification may provide clues to the extent to which the regime really is determined to pursue the objective. For some nationalities, Russification appears to be a feasible policy goal; for others, it seems virtually unattainable. One of the best indicators of Russification would be the extent of intermarriage. Unfortunately, Soviet sources provide very little data on this factor. As a result, quantitative indicators are generally limited to data on language habits: the extent to which members of a nationality group habitually speak their own language compared with the extent to which they adopt Russian for everyday usage. In this regard, it is important to note that rural inhabitants everywhere adhere to their own language, while significant numbers of urbanites adopt the "all-Union" language. To put the matter another way, the interrelation between social mobilization and Russification is intimate. But, as the Nationalities Table indicates, the relation varies enormously from nationality to nationality. One must, therefore, turn to a survey of each major group to assess its position in the Soviet system.

The Russians

The Russians are the dominant group in the U.S.S.R. Numerically, they constitute a slight majority. While the proportion of Russians who are Party members is not quite the highest, it is much higher than the proportion among the other *large* nationalities. Central Committee membership is overwhelmingly Russian, though the proportionate role of Ukrainians in the Central Committee, at least during Khrushchev's time, has been comparably large. Per capita availability of printed material in Russian is high. These indicators suggest that the regime places extraordinary reliance on the Russians, and there is a considerable amount of additional evidence that the Russian language is favored. These generalizations are borne out by historical evidence, which indicates that the Russians have constantly formed the most reliable and strongest element supporting the regime. This was particularly true during the Civil War when, for many months, Bolshevik power was virtually restricted to the Russian core areas around Moscow and Leningrad, and during World War II when most of the non-Russian population fell under German control. While Stalin was not Russian and relied, to some extent, on non-Russians in the police and the Party apparatus, key organizations like the army officer corps have always been predominantly Russian in recruitment and tradition.

One reason that the Russians have been so useful to the regime is their high degree of social mobilization, suggested by all available quantitative indicators. In a very real sense, at least until the 1950's, the cities, which are predominantly Russian in population even in many minority-nationality republics, were fortresses from which the regime dominated the countryside. As an urban, educated group, the Russians have been the backbone of the program of forced modernization.

The "Younger Brothers"

The social mobilization of the Russians stands out strongly in comparison to the other East Slavic nationalities in the U.S.S.R. Numerically, the 45 million Ukrainians and Belorussians are, next to the Russians, by far the most important nationalities. As East Slavs, they are also closest to the Russians

in language. Party membership is high among both the Ukrainians and the Belorussians; the indicators would be more
striking if one took into account the *rate of increase* of Party
membership among these nationalities since Stalin's death. In
1952, there were approximately half as many Party members
for each thousand Ukrainians and Belorussians as for each
thousand Russians; today, there are about four-fifths as many.
Similarly, proportional representation of both groups in the
Central Committee has increased from a very low level to near
parity with the Russians. These increases undoubtedly result
from the regime's desire to give symbolic recognition to Ukrainians and Belorussians, to convince them that they are really
"shareholders" in the Soviet system. All available evidence
indicates, however, that members of these groups who enter the
Party, or at least those who achieve the elite status of Central
Committee membership, are highly Russified. They habitually speak Russian and accept much of the Russian historical
tradition. As a result, the regime's policy implies *individual*
equality of opportunity for the minority East Slavs, but does
not really mean that, *as nationalities,* they are on a par with
the Russians. The indicators of printed materials strongly
support this view. As compared with the amount of material
printed in Russian, the provision of Ukrainian-language and
Belorussian-language materials is, per capita, very low. In fact,
we know that huge quantities of Russian publications are
printed in the Ukrainian and Belorussian republics, or im-
ported from the R.S.F.S.R., while only half a dozen publications in Ukrainian or Belorussian are printed outside those
republics. A similar asymmetry exists in the school situation:
Russian-language schools educate a sixth of the children in the
Ukrainian and Belorussian republics, but there are few if any
native-language schools for the substantial Ukrainian and
Belorussian minorities outside their republics. Even official
statements refer to the Russians as the "elder brothers" of the

other East Slavs. The regime's aim appears to be to draw them closer to the Russians, toward eventual assimilation.

The Belorussian group appears to present relatively slight obstacles to the "younger brother" role. The far larger Ukrainian group, on the other hand, is influenced by factors strongly impeding Russification. Historically, there has been considerable antipathy of Ukrainians toward Moscow. It is true that common adherence to the Orthodox religion led most Ukrainians to look toward the Czars in Moscow for protection. But a significant portion (now about one-eighth) of the Ukrainians, in the western region, have been Roman Catholics of the Byzantine (now Ukrainian) rite. As a distinctive religious group, the West Ukrainians opposed both the Latin-rite Catholic Poles and the Orthodox Russians. Prior to 1939, the West Ukrainians were outside the boundaries of the U.S.S.R. Nationalist organizations were so prevalent among them and so bitterly opposed to Communism and Russian domination that guerrilla activity against the Soviet regime was strong until the late 1940's. More important, perhaps, West Ukrainian nationalists, now incorporated into the U.S.S.R., still try to spread their doctrine of national independence for the Ukraine among the large majority of East Ukrainians. The regime severely represses nationalist sympathizers, but it appears that their appeal arouses memories of independence among the East Ukrainians. During the Civil War, the East Ukrainians maintained a precarious independent republic for some months. After the Bolsheviks gained control of the Ukraine, they felt obliged not only to establish a nominally separate Ukrainian Republic but, until 1930, to encourage use of the Ukrainian language in education and publication.

Probably more important as a source for Ukrainian dissatisfaction with the Moscow regime than memories of historical friction are social differences. Indicators of social mobilization clearly demonstrate the relatively low position of the Ukrainians and Belorussians. In the Ukraine and Belorussia, even more than in most other non-Russian territories, Russians (and Russian-speaking members of other nationalities) predominated in the cities during the 1920's and 1930's. Yet, that was the period when "primitive accumulation" of capital at the expense of the peasants took place. In practice, this meant that the hardships of collectivization were largely borne, in the Ukraine and Belorussia, by the native inhabitants; urban expeditions to enforce collectivization were predominantly Russian, or at least Russian-speaking. In Belorussia, the impact was not as severe as in the Ukraine, for the impoverished peasants had less to lose. The Ukraine contained, then as now, a high proportion of the best agricultural lands in the U.S.S.R. As a result, the peasants were comparatively well off. They were also more attached to individual farming, for the *mir* had never been as strong in the Ukraine as in Russian territories. Consequently, collectivization was a greater departure from tradition; as such, it was more repugnant to Ukrainians. Peasant resistance in the Ukraine was undoubtedly stronger, on the average, than in Russian rural areas. The regime's repressive measures, including wholesale banishment to Siberia and ruthless collection of harvests, was correspondingly more severe. Mass starvation decimated the Ukrainian countryside in 1933. It is not surprising that many Ukrainian peasants identified oppression, directed from Moscow and carried out by Russian-speaking city men, with Russians in general, or that, at least during World War II, Ukrainians were receptive to arguments for national independence.

As the decades have gone by, memories of collectivization undoubtedly have become less important in the Ukraine, especially to the increasing urban element. On the other hand, West Ukrainian nationalism has had some chance to spread. The post-Stalin regime has tried to enhance Ukrainian loyalty but, apart from the impeding factors just outlined, emphasis on East Slav unity is hampered by other considerations. A unified nation of Russified East Slavs would undoubtedly be extremely powerful, for it would include three-fourths of the Soviet population. The Ukraine alone provides one-fifth of the agricultural and industrial production of the Soviet Union. In terms of skills (as reflected in higher education), however, the "younger brothers" are below average. Moreover, official recognition of the dominant position of the East Slavs would have extremely serious consequences for the over-all position of the U.S.S.R. How could it continue to claim to be a multi national state, the prototype and progenitor of a future Communist commonwealth of nations? What effect would avowed Russian domination have on Soviet claims to lead world Communism or even the Communist bloc of Eastern Europe? How could Moscow justify its continued control of admittedly non-Slavic territories in a world where national independence is an almost universally popular slogan? A survey of the principal non-Slavic nationalities underscores the complexities involved in the Soviet position.

Mobilized Diasporas

Many societies that are in the transitional stage from traditional to modern include ethnic minorities that perform special functions in the social mobilization process. Such special-function minorities are geographically dispersed (hence, "diasporas") and, relative to other elements of the population, they have attained a high degree of social mobilization (hence, "mobilized diasporas"). Frequently, because social or political pressures have prevented them from following the rural occupations typical of a traditional society, these nationalities are more urban than other population elements. Mobilized diaspora members have relatively superior educational attainments, partly because education offers one of the few channels of advancement open to their minority group. Consequently,

they provide a disproportionately large share of the modernizing society's highly trained manpower (and womanpower,
because mobilized diasporas are exceptionally ready to encourage the education of their women). Mobilized diasporas are also
very valuable to modernizing societies because their members
frequently have talents in commerce, negotiation, and administration even highly educated members of the dominant
nationalities lack. These talents include a wide knowledge of
languages, which is essential to members of dispersed nationalities living among populations speaking different tongues, and
a sensitivity to human-relations problems, which minority
members must have to survive. Because of their useful quali-
ties, mobilized diasporas obtain a disproportionate share of the
key positions in a modernizing society. As the society becomes
more modernized, this apparently favored position of the minority arouses jealousy among the increasing educated stratum
of other nationalities. As a result, members of the mobilized
diaspora are frequently subject to discrimination and usually cease to perform specialized functions when the society
approaches complete modernization.

Compared to other modernized countries, Russia has had an
unusually protracted process of modernization. It began the
process in the mid-nineteenth century, roughly at the same
time as the United States. While the United States may be
considered to have basically completed the transition by about
1920, the U.S.S.R. is still, in many ways, in the latter stages of
modernization. It is not surprising, therefore, that several nationalities in succession appear to have acted as mobilized
diasporas. We have already noted the place of the Germans
among the nobility in the Czarist Empire. They were also very
prominent in administration, diplomacy, and the professions.
Since the Germans were largely displaced as a mobilized diaspora before the Revolution (though there are still nearly 2 million Germans in the U.S.S.R.), they need not be considered

further. During the Czarist period, the numerous Jews of the Empire were persecuted more severely than in any other major nation. Many Jews also suffered as a result of the disorders of the Civil War. Jewish religious life was frowned on by the Bolsheviks; Jewish businessmen eventually lost their property. Individual Jews, however, especially if they were not religious, were not discriminated against. After the Revolution, several rose to prominent positions in the Party and the state. Many other Jews (who, for the most part, preferred democratic socialism to Communism) were able to get higher educations and to move freely into skilled occupations all over the Soviet Union. Among other factors, the centuries-old urban background of most Jews and their traditional emphasis on learning made it relatively easy for them to adapt to the modernization process. As a result, in the 1920's and the 1930's, the Jews assumed an important place in Soviet society as a mobilized diaspora.

Throughout the Soviet period, every Soviet citizen of Jewish parentage, regardless of his own religious attitude, has been required to carry a passport identifying him as a Jew by nationality. The regime set this requirement partly because most Jews in the U.S.S.R. did have some characteristics of a nationality, especially in the habitual use, at the time of the Revolution, of the Yiddish language. Obviously, however, compulsory identification according to parental background paved the way for treating individual Jews as members of a group rather than in accordance with their personal attitudes and merits. This ominous potential for discrimination began to be realized in the early 1940's. Reliable reports indicate that, early in World War II, quotas setting an upper limit on the number of Jews in Party and government posts, in the arts and professions, and in higher education, were secretly decreed. In 1948–49, Yiddish cultural institutions were almost totally abolished and several prominent Jewish cultural figures were

secretly executed. In the notorious "Doctor's Plot," a predominantly Jewish group was falsely accused of atrocious crimes.
One motive for this persecution seems to have been Stalin's
personal prejudice, but, even after his death, thinly disguised
accusations of Jewish corruption and the revival of old slan-
ders against the Jewish religion suggest that anti-Semitism is
widespread. While this prejudice has many sources, one (as
Khrushchev once implied) is jealousy of the prominent role
occupied by Jews in highly skilled occupations. But, the numerous Jewish scientists, physicians, and other highly trained
personnel constitute an almost indispensable resource for the
Soviet system. Moreover, the claim of the U.S.S.R. to be a
society of brotherhood and equality is tarnished by evidence
of discrimination. Under these circumstances, the regime has
played an ambivalent game. Some indirect slurs on Jews as a
group continue to appear; Judaism is discouraged as a religion. But anti-Semitism is, occasionally, officially denounced.
Jews continue to occupy important positions, but their *proportion* in the highly skilled occupations and in university
student bodies regularly decreases. Yiddish (and Hebrew) instruction is virtually precluded; as a result, Jews have rapidly
Russified linguistically—though their rate of marriage outside
their group remains low.

With the reduced importance of the Jews as a mobilized
diaspora has come the increased importance of Armenians in
this role. As the indicators in the Nationalities Table show,
Armenians do not reach the extremely high levels of urbaniza-
tion, higher education, and skilled professional status attained
by the Jews, but the Armenians equal or exceed the Russians
in these indicators of social mobilization and are far ahead
of most other nationalities. Curiously enough, though their
women have a slightly higher indicator of educational attainment than their men, indicators of Armenian population increase remain very high. Armenians are less concentrated in

their home territory than any major nationality other than Tatars. (Jews, Germans, and Poles, who, practically speaking, have no home territory in the U.S.S.R., are not included in this comparison). Armenians are especially important as a mobilized diaspora throughout the Transcaucasus, the North Caucasus, and the Transcaspian regions. They also perform some specialized tasks in over-all Soviet institutions, especially in the area of domestic and foreign commerce. Compared to earlier mobilized diasporas, their importance may be slight; one reason for this reduction in importance of the mobilized diaspora is that Soviet society has become more modernized.

For the time being, the Armenian group enjoys certain privileges. Its distinctive Gregorian Church is subjected to less pressure than most other religious groups in the U.S.S.R.— partly because the regime tries to use it to influence the numerous Armenians living in other parts of the world. The proportion of Russians in the Armenian S.S.R. is unusually low. In some areas, Armenians outside their republic are provided with their own language schools. The relatively low per capita rate of publication in Armenian suggests that the regime does not encourage linguistic autonomy in all respects, however. At any rate, Armenians, as a highly dispersed nationality, tend, much more than most nationalities, to adopt Russian as their habitual speech. In the long run, the regime may hope to assimilate the Armenians; in the meantime, it apparently finds it worthwhile to encourage them to function as a mobilized diaspora.

The State Nations

A glance at the Nationalities Table shows that most indicators of social mobilization for the Georgians, the Estonians, and the Latvians are of the same order of magnitude as for the Russians and the Armenians. In contrast to the Armenians, however, the Georgians, Estonians, and Latvians are

highly concentrated in their home territories. Each of these
territories has, in recent times, constituted a national unit of
special strength. Between 1918 and 1939, Estonia and Latvia
were independent states with flourishing cultures and highly
developed economies. Georgia was independent for only two
years, but its favored position under Stalin, a Georgian himself, provided a kind of substitute for the cultural development and national self-confidence that is usually an attribute
of statehood. As a result, linguistic Russification has made
remarkably little progress among these three nationalities.
Much evidence suggests that a dominant tendency among
them is the determination to maintain their national identi-
ties. Consequently, we may designate these nationalities as
"state nations."

The situation of the Lithuanians and the Moldavians is
rather different. In terms of social mobilization, both nationalities rate well below the nationalities discussed so far. On
the other hand, both have a recent memory of independence
from Russia: during the interwar period, separate statehood
for the Lithuanians, and incorporation into ethnically similar
Romania for the Moldavians. Both also show a strong resistance to Russification. Consequently, it seems desirable to include them, too, among the state nations.

All of the state nations occupy highly strategic positions on
the frontiers of the U.S.S.R. Under Stalin, all except his fellow
Georgians were severely repressed, and a heavy immigration of
Russians into their republics was encouraged in order to establish what amounted to frontier garrisons of reliable elements.
The increasing strength of the U.S.S.R. has made such pre-
cautions less vital. At the same time, the regime seems to have
recognized that Russification of the state nations cannot be
accomplished quickly and that strong overt pressures in this
direction will increase dissatisfaction among them and disrupt
their significant, though minor, contribution to the Soviet

economy. As a result, a kind of stand-off appears to exist: The state-nation territories are firmly incorporated into the Soviet defensive and economic systems, but the regime permits a relatively high degree of cultural autonomy (indicated by high per capita publication rates) and a relatively low degree of political integration (suggested by low Party membership and Central Committee membership indicators) for the state nations.

Colonials

The Russian Empire, in contrast to West European colonial empires, expanded into adjoining land areas inhabited by peoples representing a gradual transition of physical types. As a result, Russians commonly do not maintain notions of racial superiority. Nevertheless, as the Russian Empire expanded into the vague borderlands of Europe and, then, into the heart of Asia itself, it absorbed nationalities that differed from the dominant Russian culture as much as the typical colony of a West European country differed from the metropolis. Even today, these nationalities, in their relatively low levels of social mobilization, resemble typical colonies. The educational and skilled occupational attainments of all seven (Azerbaidzhanis, Uzbeks, Turkmens, Kazakhs, Kirgizes, Tatars, and Tadzhiks) listed in the Nationalities Table are generally, though not universally, below those of the Soviet nationalities considered earlier in this chapter. Residential mobility appears somewhat lower, on the average, for the colonials. Their most striking difference, in the indicators of social mobilization, appears in their extraordinarily high birth rates and the great disparity between male and female educational attainment.

Both of the latter indicators reflect not only the less modernized situation of the colonials but the wide traditional cultural gap between them and other major Soviet nationalities. All of the colonial nationalities presented in the Table (as well as a number of smaller Soviet ethnic groups) were traditionally Moslem. While the Islamic faith does not require the relegation of women to agricultural and household tasks, most Moslem cultures have, in fact, put a low value on female education and discouraged women from moving into industrial and professional occupations. Even today, Soviet publications frequently complain that the persistence of these traditional attitudes associated with Islam prevent utilization of women in the work force of the once-Moslem territories.

The inferior position of women is but one of the sharply different cultural traits that persist in colonial society. The vast majority of colonials speak closely related Turkic languages. As a result, there has been considerable cultural contact and mutual cultural reinforcement among them despite the fact that the regime replaced its early efforts to set up unified Soviet Moslem republics in Central Asia and the North Caucasus with the present fragmentation along lines of minor linguistic differentiation. As the indicators suggest, the Tatars (whose home territory is adjacent to the main Russian centers) have attained educational and mobility levels closer to the Russians than to typical colonials. The Tatar educational advance predates the Revolution by generations and was accompanied by a strong nationalist and religious movement. For several decades before and immediately after the Revolution, the widely scattered Tatars played a particularly important role as educators and propagators of Turkic national feeling. Dispersed as they were, the Tatars nevertheless underwent a considerable degree of Russification. All colonial groups, however, have exhibited a high degree of resistance to linguistic Russification, while intermarriage with Slavs is almost negligible. Their children usually attend native-language schools apart from Russians. However, the relatively low levels of education for these groups has meant that publication in Turkic and in other colonial languages is not extensive on a per capita basis.

The regime has pursued a consistent policy of modernizing the Moslem societies, with notable results in terms of literacy and economic progress; this has been done despite the inflexible attitudes held by some elements of the colonial culture (such as that toward women). The regime has de-emphasized the unity of the colonial nationalities and particularly their ties with related nations (like the Iranians) outside the U.S.S.R. Correspondingly, the Soviet regime has emphasized equality of opportunity for capable members of the colonial groups and has even taken special measures to provide higher educational opportunities and access to higher positions for them. Indicators of Party membership and Central Committee membership, while not as high for colonials as for most other nationalities, would probably be much lower if the regime had not made concentrated efforts to recruit promising colonials. As with other groups, rapid upward mobility for a colonial means a measure of assimilation to the Russian culture. Apparently, however, the sense of national identity remains much stronger among upwardly mobile colonials than among persons rising from other non-Russian nationalities. This could hardly fail to be the case in view of the sharpness and duration of the distinction in cultural background. Furthermore, while we have little direct evidence of colonials' identification with national independence movements beyond the Soviet frontiers, it is most unlikely that educated persons of Moslem background would fail to draw a parallel between their own situation and that of closely related national groups in the Middle East, which have successfully asserted their independence of Europe. The situation has become more critical since Communist China denounced the Soviet Union's claim to be an Asian as well as a European state.

Under these circumstances, it is easy to see how risky it would be for the Soviet regime to emphasize East Slavic solidarity to the point of hegemony in the Soviet multinational political system. As long as the regime emphasizes its doctrinal basis and seems to be making significant progress toward Communist millennial goals, it can continue (though with uncertain success) to claim to represent the interests of the numerous non-Slavic nations. The day the Soviet regime admits the practical irrelevancy of these goals, it will stand revealed as the master of the last of the world's great colonial empires.

SUGGESTED READING • CHAPTER 6

Because the formal governmental system of the U.S.S.R. is of secondary importance, no major critical works have been devoted exclusively to it. However, most of the books listed at the end of Chapter 3 provide extensive information on Soviet government. On the other hand, a considerable number of books deal specifically with the important ramifications of nationality relations in the U.S.S.R.

ARMSTRONG, JOHN A. *Ukrainian Nationalism*. New York: Columbia University Press, 1963. A study of recent nationalist movements among the largest non-Russian group in the U.S.S.R.

BARGHOORN, FREDERICK. *Soviet Russian Nationalism*. London and New York: Oxford University Press, 1956. The most comprehensive discussion of the relation between nationalism (especially Russian) and Communism in the U.S.S.R.

BILINSKY, YAROSLAV. *The Second Soviet Republic: The Ukraine after World War II*. New Brunswick, N.J.: Rutgers University Press, 1964. A highly detailed effort analyzing Soviet policy.

CAROE, OLAF. *Soviet Empire: The Turks of Central Asia and Stalinism*. New York: St Martin's Press, 1953. The most comprehensive work devoted specifically to the Turkic peoples of Moslem background.

CURTISS, JOHN S. *The Russian Church and the Soviet State*. Boston: Little, Brown and Company, 1953. Deals mainly with the relations between the Orthodox Church and the atheism of the regime, but also has important information on Russian nationalism.

KOLARZ, WALTER. *Russia and Her Colonies*. New York: Frederick A. Praeger, 1952. A general survey of the nationality problem, especially in Soviet Asia.

PARK, ALEXANDER. *Bolshevism in Turkestan, 1917–1927*. New York: Columbia University Press, 1957. A more detailed treatment of the early contact between Communism and the Moslem Turkic group.

Pipes, Richard E. *The Formation of the Soviet Union*. Cambridge, Mass.: Harvard University Press, 1954. A very important treatment of the early relations of the Bolsheviks to the non-Russian nationalities and of the impact of this relationship on the constitutional structure of the U.S.S.R.

Reshetar, John S. *The Ukrainian Revolution*. Princeton, N.J.: Princeton University Press, 1952. The beginnings of the modern Ukrainian nationalist movement.

Schwarz, Solomon. *The Jews in the Soviet Union*. Syracuse, N.Y.: Syracuse University Press, 1951. The rise of anti-Semitism in the U.S.S.R. and its impact on the Jewish communities.

Sullivant, Robert. *Soviet Politics in the Ukraine, 1917–1957*. New York: Columbia University Press, 1962. The most comprehensive discussion of the relation between Ukrainian nationalism and Communism.

TABLE OF MAJOR NATIONALITIES OF THE SOVIET UNION

NATIONALITY	Total number in the U.S.S.R. (in thousands)	Percentage residing in home territory	Location of home territory	Linguistic group	Traditional religion	Central Committee members and alternates (1961)	Party members per thousand of nationality	Percentage of Russians in total population of home territory	Copies of books per capita published annually in national language	Number of newspapers (single printing) per capita published in national language	Number of periodicals (annual printing) per capita published in national language	Percentage under age 20	Birth rate per thousand	Percentage of nationality residing in urban areas	Urban population with more than elementary education (per thousand) Male	Female	Scientific workers (per one hundred thousand)	Specialists with higher education (per thousand)	Full-time students in higher education (per ten thousand)	Percentage of students in higher education residing in R.S.F.S.R.	Percentage of scientists residing in R.S.F.S.R.	Percentage habitually speaking native language	Percentage habitually speaking Russian	Percentage of urban population habitually speaking Russian
Russian	114,114	85	More than % of U.S.S.R.	East Slavic	Orthodox	212	64	—	9	.7	9	37	21	58	363	375	327	21	90	—	—	100	100	100
Ukrainian	37,252	86	SW Euro. U.S.S.R.	East Slavic	Ortho. & Greek Cath.	58	49	17	2	.3	1	33	21	40	426	385	159	16	60	19	29	88	12	23
Belorussian	9,914	82	W. Cen. Euro. U.S.S.R.	East Slavic	Orthodox	11	49	8	1	.15	1	36	24	33	411	399	132	14	57	29	36	84	15	36
Jewish	2,268	—	Very widely scattered	Germanic	Jewish	1	—	—	.03	.05	.01	—	—	95	686	695	2,244	142	208	—	—	22	76	78

Nationality	Population	%	Region	Language group	Religion																			
Armenian	2,787	55	Trans-caucasus	Sep-arate Indo-Euro. group	Sim. to Orth.	4	67	3	2	.2	1	40	35	57	391	394	430	30	94	13	19	90	8	14
Georgian	2,692	97	Trans-caucasus	Japhetic (obscure relation—ship)	Ortho-dox	2	74	10	4	.35	2	36	25	36	551	546	435	36	105	8	6	99	1	3
Estonian	989	90	NW Euro. U.S.S.R.	Finnic	Protestant	3	34	20	8	.7	13	26	–	47	433	437	307	22	94	12	10	95	5	7
Latvian	1,400	93	NW Euro. U.S.S.R.	Baltic	Protestant	3	32	27	7	.5	16	26	17	48	494	473	274	20	81	14	13	95	5	7
Lithuanian	2,326	93	NW Euro. U.S.S.R.	Baltic	Latin Cath.	3	26	9	5	.4	6	34	22	36	314	310	200	15	90	6	4	98	1	3
Moldavian	2,214	85	SW Euro. U.S.S.R.	Ro-mance	Ortho-dox	2	19	10	2	.2	2	41	28	13	313	246	45	6	42	9	6	95	4	19
Azerbaidzhani	2,940	84	Trans-caucasus	Turkic	Moslem (Shiite)	2	48	14	3	.2	2	46	42	35	374	248	244	18	75	10	3	98	1	3
Uzbek	6,015	84	Central Asia	Turkic	Moslem (Sunni)	7	32	14	3	.2	3	49	38	22	316	209	99	10	68	2.5	2	98	1	2
Turkmen	1,002	92	Central Asia	Turkic	Moslem (Sunni)	2	32	17	3	.3	3	46	–	25	331	202	100	12	77	11	2	99	1	2
Kazakh	3,622	77	Central Asia	Turkic	Moslem (Sunni)	3	50	43	2	.25	2	48	38	24	315	196	104	11	86	17	–	98	1	3
Kirgiz	969	86	Central Asia	Turkic	Moslem (Sunni)	2	36	30	3	.3	2	47	35	11	438	293	86	12	84	8.5	.5	99	0	2
Tatar	4,968	27	NE Euro. U.S.S.R.	Turkic	Moslem (Sunni)	1	–	44	1	.1	–	41	28	42	299	310	126	12	–	–	–	94	7	12
Tadzhik	1,397	75	Central Asia	Iranian	Moslem (Sunni)	2	30	13	3	.25	2	49	–	21	308	165	85	9	58	5	2.5	98	1	2

7

THE ADMINISTRATION
AND THE ECONOMY

For the average citizen, the crucial difference between a pluralist system and the Soviet political system is the extent to
which the regime interferes with his personal conduct. As was
discussed earlier, this interference is an essential corollary of
the Communist belief that a "new man" can be developed.
It is important to recall, however, that Marxism-Leninism
maintains that the decisive factor in creating the "new man"
does not consist of elements of the "superstructure," such as
indoctrination and police coercion, but of the "relationships
of production," which are supposed to constitute society's
"base." In the final analysis, therefore, the Soviet regime maintains that its fundamental task is the remaking of the economic environment. The outside observer may define this aim
(because it is derived from ideology rather than from consideration of efficiency) as political rather than economic; certainly,
many of the steps the Soviet regime has taken to implement it
have been motivated by purely political considerations. For
example, as was suggested in Chapter 2, the sovnarkhoz reorganization, in 1957, appears to have been heavily influenced,
if not determined, by the desire of Khrushchev's supporters to
enhance their power.

But Soviet leaders never admit such a priority of political
objectives. They insist that constructing the material foundations—first for socialism, later for Communism—has been the
principal concern of the regime. At the same time, it is obvious
that both the internal stability of the Soviet system and the influence it exerts abroad are dependent upon economic success. As
a result, economic matters receive a disproportionate amount

of the public attention of both Party and state officials. A large majority of all questions considered at Party committee plenums and congresses are economic in nature, and the amount of recorded discussion devoted to such questions is, relatively, even greater. The same is true of meetings of the Supreme Soviet and the lower soviets. While these superficial indicators of the relative importance attached to questions are unavailable for the Council of Ministers and the local executive committees, it seems safe to assume that these state bodies also devote most of their time to economic affairs. It is likely the Politburo is relatively more occupied with foreign affairs, personnel allocation, indoctrination, and other questions not directly economic in nature, but it also devotes much time to economic matters.

Indeed, a principal aspect of the eclipse of the Politburo under Stalin was the dominant role assumed by the Council of Ministers (or its committees) in directing the economy. As we have seen, the Council of Ministers lost most of these powers in the sovnarkhoz period (1957–64), but, in recent years, the Council has regained a considerable measure of importance. Compared with Stalin's time, however, the Council of Ministers remains limited by (1) the high-level decisions of the Politburo on economic as on other matters; (2) the enhanced role of lower Party organizations in agriculture; and (3) the greater leeway permitted directors of individual industrial enterprises. A thorough consideration of these developments would far transcend the scope of this book. A brief acquaintance with current developments in Soviet industrial direction is essential, however, for comprehension of the political system.

PLANNING IN THE COMMAND ECONOMY

Since its inception, the Soviet economic system has been a "command economy." In this type of system (in contrast to the "market economy" of countries like the United States), political decisions rather than "automatic" market forces are the principal method of determining what shall be produced and how it shall be allocated. At the top, decisions are made (as indicated in the preceding paragraphs) by the political bodies that exercise general control over Soviet society. They are primarily concerned with the ends for which economic production is carried on: military strength, the rate and direction of economic growth, the kinds and the levels of personal consumption. Theoretically, political decision-makers should, for the sake of efficiency, confine their directives to these economic *ends;* but in practice political bodies also interfere in the *means* by which goods are produced.

As a result, the problem of coordination of production is complicated. In principle, it has been accomplished by the somewhat rough-and-ready process known as "material balances," carried out by the State Planning Committee, or Gosplan. Briefly (if somewhat oversimplified), this means that the Soviet planners (1) determine the myriad of products that they want the economy to turn out; (2) calculate the amounts of several hundred major raw materials, semifinished parts, and pieces of equipment that will be needed to make these products;* (3) calculate the interaction in time and space between the principal elements of production needed to achieve the desired output. Until very recently, no precise calculation of these extremely intricate interactions was feasible. Instead, past experience was used as a guide, while sectors of the economy considered most important were given priority. These sectors received the best material and workmen and often overfulfilled their planned output at the expense of less favored industries. As long as the range of products was comparatively limited and the resources in raw materials and unskilled labor abundant, this system worked fairly well, as indicated by the high industrial growth rates in the U.S.S.R. during the 1930's, late 1940's, and early 1950's. As the economy became more complex

---

* The supply of less important commodities is planned at lower levels.

and sophisticated, the "slack" was taken up. Skilled labor became relatively more important, and the reduced labor supply, due to low wartime birth rates, made careful allocation of even unskilled labor resources important. The number and complexity of products and production techniques increased, and the number of interactions (a function of the square of the number of enterprises) increased enormously. As the minimal needs of personal consumption were nearly met, individual consumers became more selective. As a result of all these developments, Soviet economic planning has become seriously deficient.

Two principal avenues of improvement appear to be available. Theoretically, advanced methods of data-processing could "save" the command system. The rapid increase in the effectiveness of computer technology may provide a method for precise calculation of the enormous number of economic interactions required. "Input-output" technique employs, in effect, an enormous number of simultaneous equations to calculate the interrelation of product requirements, thereby making it possible (in theory) to command each enterprise to produce the commodities required to make supply just equal demand for all kinds of output. A more refined technique, linear programming, may even provide precise calculations concerning the effects of utilizing alternative methods or materials. Soviet economic planners have been experimenting with both methods. So far, however, it appears that the Soviet computer capacity is inadequate to handle a linear programming approach on this scale for the entire national economy. Furthermore, no technique of computer calculation is better than the data supplied. Not only is collection of economic data inadequate, but (as will appear below) the impact of the present administrative system upon the individual economic enterprise tends to generate inaccurate data.

The second alternative involves major modification of the

command economy through the adoption of features of the market economy. A relatively minor modification would be the establishment of financial criteria for the success of individual state economic enterprises. In theory, such criteria have been embodied for decades in the "economic cost accounting" (*khozraschot*) system. Each enterprise is supposed to make a monetary profit over its costs. In practice, however, volume of physical output has been a far more important criterion for judging the success of enterprises in crucial sectors like defense and machinery production. Even more important, economic cost accounting is unable to provide success indicators unless prices accurately reflect costs of production. All prices are set by the state. In consumers' goods production, the state endeavors to set these prices in accord with one principle of the market economy, the relation between supply and demand. The objective is to adjust the effective demand to the supply the regime decides should be available to consumers. For example, let us say competing priority demands for raw materials and workmen mean that only 1 million refrigerators can be manufactured. If refrigerators were to be sold at a little above production cost, potential buyers would be so numerous that the supply would soon be exhausted. The "solution" (not always successful by any means) is to set the price so high that only 1 million persons can afford refrigerators. Thus the demand is made to equal the supply. If this were the end of the matter, however, the refrigerator producer would show an enormous profit. To avoid this situation, which would reduce his incentive to operate efficiently, a "turnover tax" is placed on the item. Theoretically, the turnover tax is just large enough to cover the gap between cost of production (plus a small "planned profit") and fixed sale price. Alternatively, the turnover tax is kept low, but a large planned profit (which, of course, goes to the state just as the tax does) absorbs the difference between production cost and price to consumer. The turnover tax and the state profits on consumers' goods together are so great that they provide the Soviet state with the bulk of its revenue. Since these two items are both "hidden" taxes, they enable the regime to propagate the fiction that the average Soviet citizen pays less taxes than the citizen of any other major country.

The regime has no reason for imposing a turnover tax on goods like steel and cement, which are bought not by private individuals but by state enterprises. Moreover, the regime cannot set the price for these goods by assuming that demand should be restricted to an arbitrary amount, for the main problem confronting Soviet planners is precisely the amount of such factors of production that optimum economic production requires. In practice, therefore, the prices for most production goods have been set arbitrarily, occasionally at levels that appear to be well below the real cost of producing the goods. As a result, economic cost accounting is not very meaningful as a method for determining the efficiency of enterprises turning out production goods.

During the 1960's, Soviet economists—notably Yevsei Liberman—argued strongly for movement toward a market system. During 1964 and 1965, some steps were taken in this direction. Instead of having the nature of their product (total quantity, assortment, and quality specifications) entirely specified by the central officials, enterprise managers were permitted to engage in direct negotiations with the enterprises that used the product. Enterprise directors were instructed that they would be judged successful if their enterprises were financially profitable. Enterprise directors were also given more leeway in internal management of their plants, particularly in the kinds of labor employed and, to a limited degree, of labor incentives offered. In general, there has been a tendency to leave technical aspects of economic policy to the judgment of trained economists and practical administrators rather than to decide these matters on ideological or political grounds.

Nevertheless, the effect of the "reform" has so far been very

limited. Each enterprise is still given an over-all plan assignment. Prices recently have been revised to reflect costs more
adequately. While earlier Soviet practice failed to reflect the
cost of capital investment, various devices now permit planners to include this factor in cost accounting. Prices continue
to be administered, however, rather than determined by market forces; consequently, the financial criteria for success are
artificial. An enterprise manager can negotiate with his suppliers as well as with the enterprises that consume his product,
but he cannot be sure that the former will provide him with
the amount and quality of materials needed if he is to produce, or that the materials will arrive on schedule. Because of
the artificial price relationships, financial sanctions, which are
supposed to induce his suppliers to meet their commitments,
remain only partially effective. The Soviet regime is still un-
willing to permit prices to find their own level. One reason,
no doubt, is that, in a simulated market system, it would be
difficult to retain control over all of the ends of production.
Consumers' choices could hardly be prevented from assuming
a larger role as compared to the regime's present emphasis on
defense and industrial investment, and the kinds of goods consumers obtain could not be manipulated as readily. Another
reason is bureaucratic inertia and self-interest. We are, therefore, back to the consideration of the administrative aspects of
the system.

The enterprise manager is still subject to a wide range of
institutional controls and pressures. In the direct chain of
command, he is under a ministry (in Moscow or in a Union
republic capital) with perhaps one intermediate level of authority, the *glavk*. A major task of the ministry is to see that
the plan is fulfilled. Consequently, the ministry officials are
inclined to watch enterprises under their direction very closely
and to interfere whenever they suspect that something may
go wrong. Since most ministers (and probably their principal

subordinates) have had long experience in the centralized command economy, it is not surprising that they continue to use highly detailed plans and to issue frequent direct orders to enterprise managers. As financial considerations have become more heavily emphasized, the role of the State Bank, which acts as a superauditor for enterprises, has also become more important. Available information suggests that Bank officials carry out their supervision in a rigid manner, which further hampers the enterprise manager. Since 1964, local Party organizations have not been as directly concerned with larger enterprises as they were during the sovnarkhoz period (even then, Party officials tended to find major industrial problems too complex to deal with). In each factory, however, the primary Party organization secretary (a full-time apparatus member in large factories) transmits central pressures that often interfere with orderly processes of production.

Considering the variety of pressures he faces, it is scarcely surprising that the enterprise manager continues to resort to those irregular practices that sprang up under the unmodified command-economy system. Of these practices, one of the most important is the effort to restrict the plan assignment to a level that is below the real production capacities of his enterprise. By getting a small assignment, he is protected against failure to meet the plan and is able to show a gratifying "above-plan" output. In order to get a small assignment, he falsifies data concerning plant capacity and current output, thereby distorting the data the central planners use in their calculations. The enterprise director may also maintain an inventory of materials, in the form either of finished products or of raw materials. These inventory reserves, being unknown to the central planners, further distort their calculations. If they are not utilized, the inventories also constitute unproductive capital. However, in many cases the inventories do not remain unutilized. Because of the difficulty of enforcing the commitments of suppliers, many enterprise managers employ special expediters (*tolkachi*). The job of the *tolkachi* is to induce suppliers to meet their schedules or, if this fails, to find available supplies that the plan did not allocate to the expediters' enterprises. Obviously, the most likely source of such unplanned supplies are concealed inventories in other enterprises. If an expediter's enterprise also has a concealed inventory, a mutually beneficial barter deal may be arranged.

The practices described in the preceding paragraphs are entirely illegal and the clandestine atmosphere in which they occur facilitates chicanery for personal gain. They do, however, provide a measure of flexibility in the command economy, which is probably indispensable even after the modest "Liberman" reforms. As long as an enterprise manager is successful in meeting his planned production assignment and avoids involvement with unsuccessful political factions, his resort to these extralegal practices is apt to be overlooked. In recent years, even Soviet press accounts contain wry admissions that the *tolkachi* and the hidden inventories may serve the ends of the economic system as a whole. If, however, the manager is clearly unsuccessful or in political disfavor, his illegal practices can become the basis for serious charges. In Stalin's time, such charges resulted in death or long imprisonment. Today, such severe penalties for economic derelictions that do not involve embezzlement or speculation are uncommon, but the least a disgraced manager could expect would be reduction to a low-paying and obscure position.

On the whole, the Soviet industrial system has been successful so far. During World War II, the capacity of industry to resume production after evacuation from areas threatened by the Germans was almost miraculous. The over-all growth rate has been extremely impressive. In recent years, however, this rate has slowed considerably. Labor efficiency is low compared to that common in the United States and the quality of many manufactured goods and of much construction is shoddy. Undoubtedly, the U.S.S.R. can produce items such as rockets or jet airplanes technically equal or superior to any others in the world. Apparently, however, only a fairly narrow range of Soviet industry can attain such standards. In "normal" times, the regime uses this sector of industry for the highest-priority items. But it is still doubtful whether Soviet industry as a whole has the capacity for vast expansion of output of items requiring extremely high technical standards of production.

AGRICULTURE

In terms of over-all production, Soviet agriculture presents a picture almost opposite to Soviet industry. In contrast to the slowdown in industrial growth, recent agricultural production increases have been encouraging, but the over-all record of agriculture is greatly inferior to the industrial growth record. While countries as diverse in background as the United States and Japan increased their crop yields enormously between 1913–53, Soviet food production in the mid-1950's remained almost the same as it had been in 1913. During the late 1950's and early 1960's, various measures introduced by Khrushchev—such as the "virgin lands" program of exploitation in arid regions—led to a growth spurt, but the situation greatly worsened in 1963. In 1964–66, however, food production (mainly grains) exceeded all previous records, even on a per capita basis.

The very mixed record of Soviet agriculture is undoubtedly due in part to adverse climatic conditions. Most of the U.S.S.R. has extremely severe winters and short growing seasons, while the southern parts of the country are largely arid. Limitations of capital and human resources are also very important; these limitations are undoubtedly dependent, at least in large part, on the regime's policies. Until very recently, the Soviet regime gave a high priority to heavy industry in terms both of capital investments and of the assignment of skilled personnel. Agriculture, like other consumers' goods sections, tended to receive only those resources left over after industry was taken care of (a notable exception was "technical-crop" farming—fibers, sugar beets, et cetera—which made rapid progress even under Stalin). Drainage of the numerous swampy areas was neglected. The infrastructure of farm-to-market roads was primitive, and chemical fertilizers and insecticides were very scarce. A considerable amount of heavy farm machinery (tread tractors, combines) was supplied, but small, flexible mechanical implements were not made available or could not be properly maintained. It appears that much of the very recent grain increase is due to drainage measures and the provision of chemical fertilizer, but the road and implement problems remain unsolved.

Probably more important than capital-equipment deficiencies are the social problems confronting Soviet agriculture. In 1929, Stalin launched a campaign for total collectivization of farming. The campaign took a heavy toll—approximately 5 million deaths. Many of these were "kulaks" (officially defined as "richer" peasants employing hired labor, but in practice taken to mean all those who resisted either passively or actively) or their families, shot or exiled to Siberia. Other peasants died in the famine that followed the disruption of agricultural operations. Loss of livestock, while less horrifying, had a profoundly depressing effect on the development of Soviet agriculture. Two-thirds of the sheep and goats, half of the swine and horses, and one-third of the cattle were lost between 1929 and 1933. The number of cattle did not reach the 1929 figure until 1958.

It appears that Stalin's principal motivation for the drastic collectivization campaign was political control of the peasantry, who up to then had been less affected by Communist indoctrination than any other major segment of the population. The regime has never relaxed its grip on the countryside, but the instrumentalities of control have varied considerably. Until 1958, major instruments were the MTS (machine tractor stations), which operated most of the heavy agricultural machinery, thereby dominating the planting and harvesting operations. The MTS were agencies of the Ministry of Agriculture, but during much of Stalin's life their key political sections were controlled by the police agencies. Even at that time, however, the local Party organizations (especially the raikoms) exercised far more control over agriculture than over industry. Khrushchev secured for the local Party an almost complete ascendancy over state organizations when it came to agricultural control. During the Khrushchev period, the MTS were abolished and their machinery "sold" to the collective farms. At the same time, consolidation of collective farms and the spread of rural Party membership made it possible to establish primary Party organizations on nearly every farm. Since 1964, the raikom and the primary Party organizations have remained the most important rural control agencies, but the Ministry of Agriculture has regained influence. Like the industrial ministries, the Ministry of Agriculture has the task of seeing that its economic branch—the collective farms and the state farms (which are especially important in the production of technical crops) —meets its quotas. As an aid in accomplishing this task, the Ministry directly supervises a broad network of experimental stations, agricultural specialists, and veterinaries.

The Kolkhoz

Since 1929, the agricultural artel, known more commonly as the kolkhoz or collective farm, has been by far the most important form of agricultural organization in the U.S.S.R.

Today, about 75 per cent of the peasants are in kolkhozes. Most of the remainder are in state farms (the sovkhozes). On the 10,000 sovkhozes, workers are paid wages like factory hands. The 38,000 kolkhozes, on the other hand, are in theory cooperatives rather than state enterprises. The average kolkhoz has some 420 families and about 9,000 acres of cultivated land. The collectivized fields include most of the cultivated areas and produce the bulk of major food crops, such as grain and potatoes. Most larger types of livestock are also raised in collective herds. Every able-bodied member of the collective farm —women and men, adolescents and adults—must work a fixed minimum of days (nearly 300 in the case of able-bodied men) in the collective "sector" of the farm.

Obviously, the success of Soviet agriculture depends to a large extent upon the efficiency attained in cultivating the collective sector. The official directly responsible is the chairman, nominally elected by the members of the farm, but actually designated by the Party. It is the chairman's job to see that the kolkhoz produces the kind and amount of products set for it in the state plan and that produce deliveries are made to the state on schedule. A major problem is stimulation of the peasants' efforts. Most industrial workers are under a piece-work system, which rewards each according to his output; it is, however, harder to evaluate the peasants' performance of agricultural tasks. The usual system was to set a fixed number of labor days (*trudodni*) for a real day spent at a given task. Thus a skilled agricultural-machine operator might receive two labor days for each day actually worked, while an elderly woman might get only one-half a labor day for a full day spent in the poultry yard. While various bonus systems were tried, all workers performing a given task on the same kolkhoz tended to receive the same labor-day credit, regardless of their efficiency. Probably even more important was the fact that the labor day did not have a fixed cash value. At the end of the crop year, the collective farm sold much of its produce to the state at fixed prices. Some of the produce was stored for seed or reserve. The remainder was sold on the free market or distributed to the collective members in proportion to their accumulation of labor days, as was any cash surplus the farm might have after paying its expenses. No one knew in advance how much these distributions in cash or kind might be, nor was there any apparent justice in the allocation. A collective farm fortunate enough to have good soil and a good location provided far higher rewards for its members than another with equally efficient farmers but less favorable conditions, and all were dependent on the whims of the weather. Under these circumstances, the individual collective farmer had little incentive to devote his best efforts to the collectivized sector. Instead, he tended to concentrate his efforts upon the backyard "garden plot" assigned to him and his family.*

As a kind of personal enterprise, garden-plot farming has always been suspect by the regime. Moreover, from the purely practical standpoint, labor devoted to these gardens tends to be diverted from collectivized agriculture. Stalin and Khrushchev repeatedly sought to curb the garden plots, most drastically in the *agrogorod* scheme of 1950–51, which would have brought the peasants together in large "agricultural cities" and required them to sell most of their livestock to the collective farms. The scheme seemed designed to prevent the peasant from sneaking time from his collective assignments to tend his garden, which would have been situated far from his house. Moreover, peasants grouped in compact settlements could be more easily subjected to political control and indoc-

---

* These plots average only a little more than one-half acre. Nevertheless, they provide most of the peasant's fruit and vegetables, and even some grain. With the help of grain distributed from the collectivized sector, the peasants have been able to produce in these "gardens" an astounding proportion of the animal products of the U.S.S.R. As late as 1964, two-fifths of the Soviet milk and meat and three-fourths of the eggs were produced on these family plots.

trination. Nevertheless, after much discussion in the press and some experimentation on the farms, the scheme was given up. Evidently the regime discovered that peasant resentment made the danger of another catastrophic disruption of agricultural production too great. After Stalin died, Khrushchev resumed some tentative steps toward eliminating personal garden plots, but was apparently afraid to press the matter to conclusion.

Since Khrushchev's removal, the Soviet leaders have tried quite different tactics. Garden-plot farming has been encouraged and the collective-farm markets in urban centers have been improved. In these markets, peasants may dispose of the surplus from their gardens by bargaining with purchasers. These islands of free marketing are highly successful, for the city population obtains a high proportion of its food in them.

Khrushchev greatly reduced the financial burdens on the peasants by lowering taxes and increasing the prices the state paid for crop deliveries. The current leadership has taken several major steps to improve incentives for labor in the collectivized sector. A very recent decree (May, 1966) calls on the collective farms to guarantee each farmer an annual wage not lower than that received by the corresponding state-farm employee. State Bank credits are provided to make these guarantees feasible. Moreover, the peasant now receives cash advances at intervals throughout the year, instead of having to wait for an annual distribution of profits. The large brigade, which performed most of the work on the collectivized fields between 1947 and 1964, is being replaced, to a considerable extent, by the small team (the "link" or *zveno*). Distribution of farm profits (if there are any after the fixed wages are covered) will apparently be made in accordance with the production achieved by each team. Members of the team know each other well (frequently, families work together) and therefore can put pressure on laggards to work more efficiently.

It seems unlikely that these recent measures have had an

effect on the rapid rise of grain production in the U.S.S.R. in 1965 and 1966; more likely, a combination of good weather and a relatively abundant supply of fertilizers is responsible. Soviet leaders are increasingly optimistic about their chances of solving the problem of agricultural growth, however. It remains to be seen whether the peasant will respond adequately. Even if he is impressed by the new incentives, his skills are low. The farm work force includes a higher proportion of women, elderly persons, and adolescents than does the urban; as a result, the level of education and technical training is low. With the best of will, these farm workers will have difficulty in handling the increasingly complicated mechanical devices needed for efficient farming. For example, as late as 1962, only 25 per cent of the cows could be milked by machine, apparently because maintenance of the machines was inadequate. At the same time, the huge force required to perform Soviet farm work contributes to the general labor shortage. Kolkhoz peasants constitute 24 per cent of the Soviet work force and another 9 per cent are employed in state farms and other agencies engaged in agricultural activities. In fact, it is only the large-scale employment in the urban work force of mothers of young children that enables the U.S.S.R. to make up for the waste of labor in farming.

The renewed stress on garden plots, small work teams, and incentives, represents a retreat from the movement toward full Communism. Even if the new measures result in economic benefit for the Soviet system, it is by no means certain that they will end peasant discontent. Relaxation of controls over their individual activity may, indeed, whet their appetites for more land and more freedom to cultivate it. There is little doubt that the peasantry has been the least socialized element of the population in terms of acceptance of Communist ideology; small work teams based on the family make it more difficult to carry on indoctrination. Inarticulate and dis-

organized as they are, the peasants hardly constitute a threat
to the regime. However, most of the disaffected nationality
groups are also predominantly peasant in social composition.
In time of crisis, articulation of the peasants' latent hostility
by nationalist appeals could pose a real danger to the Communist system.

SUGGESTED READING • CHAPTER 7

Many of the general works on the Soviet system listed in earlier
chapters have sections dealing with economic affairs, especially in
their administrative and political aspects. The following works are
more particularly concerned with the economy.

BAYKOV, ALEXANDER. *The Development of the Soviet Economic System.* New York: The Macmillan Company, 1947. The most complete treatment of the development of the economy and economic
administrative institutions up to the end of World War II.

BERLINER, JOSEPH. *Factory and Manager in the U.S.S.R.* Cambridge,
Mass.: Harvard University Press, 1957. A fascinating study (based
largely on interviews with émigrés who had once held managerial
posts in Soviet industry) of the problems and personalities of
Soviet directors.

BIENSTOCK, GREGORY, *et al. Management in Russian Industry and
Agriculture.* London and New York: Oxford University Press,
1944. An older but very interesting survey of the whole economic
management system.

CAMPBELL, ROBERT W. 2d ed. *Soviet Economic Power: Its Organization, Growth and Challenge.* Boston: Houghton Mifflin Company,
1966. A very clear and readable summary, available in paperback,
of the basic economic features of the U.S.S.R.

GRANICK, DAVID. *Plant Management in the Soviet Industrial System.*
New York: Columbia University Press, 1954. A monographic study
of the backgrounds and practices of managers in the 1930's.

————. *The Red Executive.* New York: Doubleday and Company,
1960. A very interesting study of the industrial manager based
on published materials and the author's observations in the
U.S.S.R., with a wealth of comparative material from Western
Europe and the United States.

JASNY, NAUM. *The Socialized Agriculture of the U.S.S.R.* Stanford, Calif.: Stanford University Press, 1949. A massive discussion of the evolution of collectivized agriculture until the postwar period.

LAIRD, ROY D. *Collective Farming in Russia: A Political Study of Soviet Kolkhozy.* Lawrence, Kan.: University of Kansas Press, 1958. A comprehensive study of the political aspects of Soviet agriculture in the early Khrushchev period.

NOVE, ALEC. Rev. ed. *The Soviet Economy: An Introduction.* New York: Frederick A. Praeger, 1966. An excellent, concise treatment, available in paperback, by a leading British economist.

SCHWARTZ, HARRY. *Russia's Soviet Economy.* Englewood Cliffs, N.J.: Prentice-Hall, 1954. The best general survey of the Soviet economy, with special emphasis on the growth and distribution of production facilities.

U.S. CONGRESS, JOINT ECONOMIC COMMITTEE. *Comparisons of the United States and Soviet Economies.* Washington, D.C.: U.S. Government Printing Office, 1960. An extremely useful set of three pamphlets consisting of articles and statistical analyses by experts.

VOLIN, LAZAR. *A Survey of Soviet Russian Agriculture.* Washington, D.C.: U.S. Government Printing Office, 1951. A slim pamphlet prepared by a government expert; rather old now, but still unsurpassed for concise, clear, and reliable presentation.

8

A SUMMING UP

It would be rash to assert that the expectations men have about politics play a more significant part in the Soviet system than in other political systems. Part of the apparent importance of Soviet political culture may arise from our inability to examine attitudes and personality structures in the U.S.S.R. directly. Nevertheless, at least from our limited perspective, the amalgam of Russian heritage and Marxist-Leninist ideology appears to have an enormous effect on behavior, particularly among the elite.

We have deliberately avoided any effort to describe in detail the link between the elements of the Russian heritage described in Chapter 1 and the specific features of the Soviet system. That such a connection exists is generally conceded, but few students of Russian history would agree on the exact way in which the heritage has influenced the present. One may assume that the tradition of subordinating the individual to the group—whether through the official despotism of the Czarist regime, the customs of the peasant *mir,* or the left-wing insistence on art for revolution's sake—has facilitated the imposition of Soviet totalitarianism. In Lenin's reinterpretation of Marxism we seem to see a direct influence (though possibly a subconscious one) of the Russian background. Sociological studies have shown that descendants of the pre-Revolution educated strata have been able, on the whole, to obtain places in the Soviet intelligentsia. One can expect, therefore, that the attitudes current in these strata have been passed on. However, like all great societies, Czarist Russia contained many contradictory elements; consequently, sweeping generalizations about its influence on the present are unwarranted. Despite these cautions, it *is* important for the student to realize that the present Soviet system has not been imposed on a blank slate.

The Marxist-Leninist component of contemporary Soviet political culture seems more evident. If one accepts the declarations of the regime at their face value, the ideology is the core of the system. Nor does the fact that major elements of the ideology have been altered and re-altered by Lenin's successors negate this assumption, for Marxism-Leninism has always stressed the need for continual interaction of theory and practice. As the Soviet elite has changed, the psychological force of the doctrine has correspondingly altered. The Bolshevik revolutionary, dedicated to destroying the old order so as to be able to proceed to the rapid construction of a perfect society, has long since been replaced by the Party bureaucrat. Until recently, at least, the latter was able to find a connection between his personal progress from obscurity to power and the material accomplishments and enhanced prestige of the regime. The successes of the Soviet regime seem narrow and philistine to many in the outside world and, apparently, to many sensitive persons in the U.S.S.R. To the officials who form the backbone of the regime, however, its achievements have been great enough to bolster their faith in the eventual fulfillment of the Marxist prophecy of the triumph of Communism. But, since 1961, this belief has suffered a number of severe shocks. Probably the most severe were set-backs in the international arena—the forced withdrawal of Soviet missiles from Cuba and the open rupture with China. Because the historical inevitability of the spread of Communism throughout the world is a fundamental Leninist tenet, these reversals imply, at the least, an indefinite postponement of the millennial goals. Soviet statements continue to stress that the current line of "peaceful coexistence" does not mean the abandonment of the drive for world Communism—only the application of different tactics. But it is hard to believe that the elite itself is as convinced of its ultimate success as was the case six years ago.

The past six years have seen the development of what may be an even more fundamental danger for Marxist-Leninist ideology. In 1961, for the first time in the history of the Communist movement, a fairly definite timetable for attaining the millennial goals was set. Along with this timetable went a series of prescriptions for transitional measures during the following twenty years. A third of this time has elapsed, but many of the prescriptions, such as limitations on farmers' garden plots, opposition to personally owned housing and automobiles, and the use of "collective" bodies for enforcing discipline, have been abandoned. The regime still insists on the necessity of eventually eliminating private property, material incentives, and state coercive agencies, but there is little or no reference to a timetable for accomplishing this. The regime appears to hold as firmly as ever, however, to one basic element of the materialist aspect of Communist ideology—atheism. Belief in science as a force that, under Communist control, can explain and accomplish everything fits in neatly with the concept of Marxism-Leninism as the supreme science of society and with the Communist official's self-image as an engineer of society. Just as obviously, this creed of materialism rules out transcendental belief; there is no clear evidence that attacks on religion in the U.S.S.R. have abated.

The place of the Party also seems secure in the minds of those who accept the ideology. Indeed, the ouster of Khrushchev (which may have been a consequence of waning confidence in the attainment of millennial goals) probably reinforced the symbolic importance of the Party as such. While there has been some increase in the operational importance of state institutions in the past three years, the role of the Party as a legitimizing institution is indispensable for the present elite. Without an individual leader to symbolize the system, its central institution must be emphasized. Probably the tacit abandonment of the 1961 Party program goals also makes it seem necessary to cling to the institutional forms of the Party. The fact that the life experiences of the present elite (at the Central Committee and at the Politburo level) are grossly out of line with life experiences of the general Party membership and of the population as a whole reinforces the elite's eagerness to cling to Party orthodoxy. Most oligarchies have been conservative rather than dynamic, and an aged oligarchy is even more likely to be orthodox rather than innovative. At the same time, the lack of overt clashes during Khrushchev's dismissal and the surface harmony among his successors may well have convinced the elite that they have found mechanisms for avoiding the succession crises that formerly racked the Soviet system. Avoidance of drastic policy innovations, which reduces the scope of debate and differences among the elite, may make it easier to cope with the next succession. All of these factors suggest a period of retrenchment.

Within a few years, however, advanced age will compel the present elite to cede power to a new generation. Whether the latter will move from orthodox conservatism to reliance on a more pragmatic ideology, or whether a younger elite will seek to restore the dynamic aspects of Communism can only be a matter for speculation. In either case, the new elite generation will face problems that may undermine the stability of the Soviet system. Overt departure from Marxism-Leninism would make it hard to justify continued rule of non-Russians by Moscow, to say nothing of the effect it would have on the Soviet regime's position in Eastern Europe. On the other hand, memories of the unfulfilled promises of 1961 will make it difficult to reinspire enthusiasm for the development of the "new man" of the Communist millennium.

Under Stalin's dictatorship, lack of enthusiasm among the Russian peasantry and more extreme disaffection among other national groups could be met by overwhelming force. In many ways, it was the availability of modern technology that made totalitarian control and indoctrination possible at that time. Large forces armed with modern weapons made effective resistance impossible, while the railroad network was used to shift uprooted populations to remote agricultural frontiers or to primitive quarters in the industrial centers. Utilizing modern means of communication and its ubiquitous security police, Stalin's regime in Moscow rooted out disaffection in 8 million square miles of territory. The printing press (and, to a lesser extent, the radio) made it possible quickly to transmit a uniform "line" to the army of propagandists and agitators. And the enormous cloacae of concentration camps silently eliminated the human "waste" that the regime felt the Soviet system could not expediently absorb. It is conceivable that a new elite could utilize similar methods for a short time. But, for all its defects, Stalin's regime retained the allegiance of an elite that equated its own success with the material successes of the system and was willing to undergo great hardships as well as to impose brutally harsh sacrifices upon the mass of the population. Considerable elements, especially workers in the Russian cities, continued to believe in the goals of Communism and to accept the means used to attain them. The limited consensus supporting coercion, rather than coercion itself, was the ultimate basis for Stalin's rule. It is most doubtful that a new elite could find even a limited consensus to serve as a basis for widespread and long-lasting coercion. If a new elite cannot do this, it may have to retreat to a territorially restricted Russian nation-state with a mixed economy and a stratified social system not markedly different from those prevailing in other modernized countries. In such a case, pressures for a pluralist political system would probably be strong, but we lack historical parallels to indicate whether or not such pressures in a modernized society could be resisted by a determined oligarchy. On the other hand, it is always possible that the Soviet elite can achieve a break-through that will reinvigorate faith in millennial goals. The extent of the economic progress needed to constitute such a break-through is incalculable, though it scarcely seems attainable in the next few years. A resounding Soviet success in international affairs, which seemed to bring world Communist domination in sight, might have the same reinvigorating effect. Quite possibly, therefore, the ultimate development of the Soviet system will be decided not by its own members but by those who anxiously observe it from afar.

INDEX